FUN WITH SKITS,
STUNTS, AND STORIES

D1562599

FUN WITH SKITS, STUNTS, AND STORIES

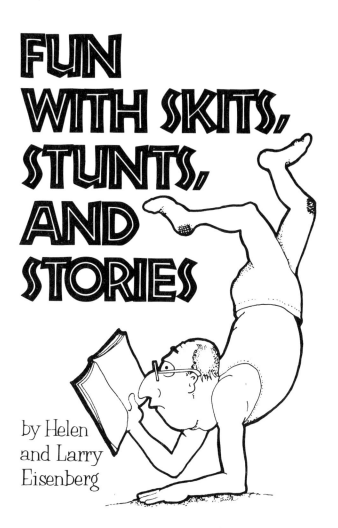

by Helen
and Larry
Eisenberg

BAKER BOOK HOUSE
Grand Rapids, Michigan

First reprinted 1975 by Baker Books
a division of Baker Book House Company
P.O. Box 6287, Grand Rapids, MI 49516-6287
with permission of Association Press

Library of Congress Catalog Card Number: 55-7411

ISBN: 0-8010-3367-5

Mass market edition
Sixteenth printing, January 1995

Printed in the United States of America

CONTENTS

Foreword, 9

1

There's Fun for Everybody and Every Occasion, 12
   skits, stunts, and stories—for whom and for what . . . how to
   prepare for skits and stunts . . . where to find skit and stunt ideas

2

Stunts and Stories? Let's Try 'Em, 26
   stunts for the leader alone . . . stunts for leader and group . . .
   stories read by the leader . . . when the group joins in the story

3

Have You Heard About Quickies, 76
   short skits and stunts

4

Can You Do This, 126
   feats . . . forfeits and initiation stunts

FOREWORD

S OCIAL recreation groups have demonstrated to us their need for skit and stunt material by the gracious reception of our earlier volume, *The Handbook of Skits and Stunts.*

In *Fun with Skits, Stunts, and Stories* we are including humorous stories as well. For many years we have had gratifying success in the use of humorous stories to be read aloud, and so we commend them to you.

Most authors are indebted to many people in getting out a collection of material, and we are no exceptions. Many of these ideas have been shared, by word of mouth, by persons whose identity has now slipped our minds. We are especially grateful to these folk for their contributions in various ways: Jameson Jones, Howard Tanner, Nina Reeves, Mrs. Chris Brown, Wally Chappell, Warren Willis, Ed Schlingman, Maurice Bone, Bob Tully, Joan Daly, George Harper, Tillie Bruce, Mrs. R. A. Bechtel, R. Bruce Tom, F. L. McReynolds, the Buckeye and Hoosier Recreation Laboratories and the Graduate Workshop at the University of Indiana, Hoover Rupert, Kermit Long, Cubby Whitehead, Buford Bush, Ford Lippold, Bob Blount, Jr., Sibley Burnett, Howard Ellis, Paul Weaver, Barbara Tyler, Paul Jackson, and all those whose names appear in this volume.

We appreciate also the co-operation of those publishers who have kindly granted the use of material from their books, as indicated in the credit lines.

HELEN AND LARRY EISENBERG

chapter 1

THERE'S FUN FOR

EVERYBODY

AND EVERY

OCCASION

for whom and for what?
how to prepare for skits and stunts
where to find skit and stunt ideas

THE TELEPHONE rang, and there was an anxious voice on the other end: "You've got to help me, for I haven't the slightest idea what to do. I'm in a spot, and I'm desperate!"

"What spot?"

"I'm responsible for the fellowship in a meeting that's going dead if we don't have some fun early in the program. I don't know what to do!"

After the caller had jotted down a few ideas given him on the telephone, he said with relief, "Why, that sounds simple. Anybody could do those things. You've saved my life!"

A few skits and stunts, used at the proper time, may not save a life, but they may save a program or a meeting from being colorless and deadly boring.

Skits, stunts, and stories, if properly used, can help greatly to liven a meeting and to make group life more enjoyable. Many of them call for both individual and total group participation. They radiate the spirit of group fun. If imagination is drawn upon, they can reflect real, creative ingenuity, especially when they bring in ideas and items of local interest. By poking fun at outgrown organizational and group procedures, skits and stunts may help to change such practices for the better. Many organizations have discovered, too, that they can sell ideas through clever skits and stunts.

To indicate the scope of this book, we give you these five categories (though they may not appear in the order named here):

1. The physical feat and trick. Some people regard these

activities as stunts, and so we have included a number of them.

2. The brief dramatic sketch or joke which features a punch line. This "quickie" moves toward a surprise climax, and it is often ended with a "blackout" (turning the lights out briefly to indicate the end) or a quick curtain.

3. The complete dramatic skit which takes a longer time to develop and calls for a little more rehearsal than a "quickie."

4. A tricky, enjoyable game or activity—such as a table stunt or a musical stunt—which is unusual enough to provide an appeal beyond that of an ordinary game.

5. The entertaining type of longer story which may be offered to the group for relaxation and amusement by the leader or another good reader.

The stories included in this book are mostly in the "quickie" category. The authors have found them very useful for breathers, times of relaxation, and general group entertainment. Though this compilation provides, for the most part, humorous material, some of it is serious.

SKITS, STUNTS, AND STORIES—
FOR WHOM AND FOR WHAT?

Skits, stunts, and stories are tailor-made for many kinds of situations. For instance, to introduce the faculty of an informal group (like a camp or a short-term training school) let them do Rhythmic Spelling, or an improvised school scene, using Boners. To "warm up" a group, or for fun during a meeting, or as a filler for a break of any kind, try some of the audience-participation stunts in the one-person and "quickie" sections.

To get participation from a large group, use a narrator stunt, with one person reading and the others acting, as in

"The Chartreuse Murder Case." For a light chapel program, try some "quickies" and short stories. For camp fun and fellowship, use almost any of the types mentioned, but particularly the feats, stories, and honoring stunts.

If a problem comes up in group life, the way to solve it may be to do a skit that lays out the problem (sometimes exaggerating it humorously) and then to have a discussion, sometimes in several groups of five or six persons each, with a summary of findings at the end. Stunt nights in organizations provide a framework for fun and participation. Almost any of the stunts—especially the longer ones—would be good there.

Parties large and small provide an excellent opportunity for using practically everything in the book, especially the one-person stunts, "quickies," and stories. To close a home party sometime, take twenty minutes to read "Cast Up by the Sea," for a delightful time in a mellow mood.

One way of developing group fellowship is for the group to start "pulling things." Stunts and tricks done in good spirit add more fun to the already present spirit of fun. At the table in camp, for instance, young people have fun with just such "bright" remarks as this (all reciting aloud together): "Bob Mitchell's table is SO DUMB that it thinks Wallace Chappell is a place where church meets."[1] At the next meal (or perhaps at the same one) Bob Mitchell's table answers in similar vein.

Other tables have done "knock-knocks" in the same fashion, by calling out together the name of a person or a delegation on the other side of the dining room, then going through the "knock-knock" routine, such as these quips: "Amos—a mosquito bit me"; "Andy—and he bit me again"; "Utah—you talk too much."

Wise leadership in any group, for young or old, will try to minimize or stop the use of tricks, stunts, "smart sayings,"

[1] From George Harper, Great Falls, Mont.

and particularly "goat stunts" if they tend to get out of hand. Laughter is an important part of the expression of group fellowship, but "laughing with" instead of "laughing at" is the aim of the thoughtful group and group leader.

Another clever use of stunts and skits is to work out a special setting around which several features may be presented. In a stunt night an ingenious leader[2] did "The Saga of Red Riding Hood." The story was told in several ways: in the Spoonerism style of Colonel Stoopnagle; in the German dialect of Dave Morrah, "Reddish Riden Hood"; in the Dragnet record, a take-off on Riding Hood and the television program. At the outset the leader told the story straight, and then he demonstrated all these other ways of telling the story—to the delight of the audience. (See *The Handbook of Skits and Stunts* for the Stoopnagle version, "Little Ride Hooding Red.")

Honoring People. A delightful way to honor members of the group is to put on a skit or stunt, then perhaps to make an award or give recognition. Sometimes this fun may be a take-off on the person, done, of course, in good humor. Everyone likes surprises, and if they are carried out in a kindly sort of humor, they can bring great delight to the persons honored.

Instead of merely singing "Happy Birthday," for example, the group might get some of its members to act out a yarn about a person who tried to get his birthdays stopped. Why? So that he could handle that crowd of nincompoops he had to work with . . . his strength was failing. Who are these people? He tells the examiner. "Oh, well," says the examiner in this Birthday Court of Appeals, "I know that crowd myself. After this birthday you won't have to have any others!" Then the entire crowd sings "Happy Birthday."

Sometimes the group will ask the person who is to be

2 Harold Hipps, Greensboro, N. C.

honored to come up front and make a report or perform in some way, and then, to the person's complete surprise, it gives him a present, sings a song in his honor, or otherwise makes recognition. Anniversaries are quite as important as birthdays.

"This Is Your Life" is another delightful, "sobby" way to honor someone. Taking their cue from the airlanes, some groups actually dig into a person's past and get people to come from some distance to be there for the event. Care should be taken to keep the occasion from getting maudlin.

One group, in wishing to present a musical instrument to one of its number, asked him to come forward and play a tune or two on the instrument (he had just recently learned to play one). He performed, and then he was told by a group representative that it was his instrument now!

Promotional Stunts. Stunts for what as well as for whom, you ask? Well, how about putting on a stunt or a skit to promote something your club or group is trying to do? Breathes there any organization without something to promote? If the group is breathing at all, it has some emphasis to be highlighted, a publication to be plugged, or some indifferent members that need just the kind of a shot-in-the-arm that a humorous skit can give. Here is the way one group of high school and college young people worked this out in a church summer camp.

The Fixit Clinic[3]

CHARACTERS: Two attractive nurses: Miss Hypo Dermic and Miss Lower Dermic; their secretary, Miss Taka Letter (who brings in the patients); and Dr. Know-It-All. There is a panel of consultants.

SCENE: Doctor's office with sign, "Office Hours—from Here to Eternity." Operating table with lantern, a camera for

[3] Mrs. Merthel Nay, Cary, Miss.

"hexed ray" pictures, an iron (for ironing out the difficulty or for pressing matters), darts (for hypodermic needles), scissors, knives, hammers, horseshoes, rubbing alcohol, and assorted organizational publications. On the wall are "stethoscopes" (bent coathangers). A tennis racquet on a suitcase serves as the "mike." There are also signs, "On the Air."

At the outset it is explained that this "TV" program is designed to help patients with such troubles as indigestion of materials, low member pressure, poorly functioning committees, decaying officers, extinguished members, loose livers, poisoned programs, and giving-pains.

The theme song, adapted to the points to be gotten across, can be written to the music of "The Campbells Are Coming":

"We're bringing a program to you today

So listen quite closely to all we say. . . . "

Patients then begin streaming in with "questionitis." The secretary ushers them in, making such remarks as "This disease is catching, I do believe," and "Great greasy goosehoppers—here comes another!" "What'll we try on this one—artificial perspiration?"

The doctor is busy, of course, diagnosing ailments and prescribing literature. Some prescriptions are given over the telephone. The questions that the "sick" are asked are connected with the work of the organization and its setup.

Commercials interspersed are like these: "If you don't feel good, try those five delicious flavors at the canteen and elsewhere: orangeade, arcade, first aid, ladies' aid, and bandaid brands of Organization Pep." "We interrupt this program to bring you some HOT NEWS. FLASH!" (A match is lighted quickly.) Others are of the nature of those found in Chapter 4 and also in *Skit Hits.*

At the end, after appropriate words, the cast announce

that they are "off." Then they sign "Off" on a blackboard, and walk out.

HOW TO PREPARE FOR SKITS AND STUNTS

Many skits and stunts call for some kind of advance preparation if they are to be smoothly and convincingly done. By all means, get the cast together and practice as long as is needed.

Timing the Stories. For any "read aloud" material, timing is important, since most of the stories used are humorous ones. One of the first things an actor learns is to "hold for laughs"—that is, he must stop completely to let the audience enjoy the "punch line" of a joke, or to let the full import of a pun or a boner "soak in." Skillful comedians develop some kind of "business" to do while people are laughing—such as taking a drink of water, mopping the forehead, adjusting eyeglasses, or turning a page. Some performers will look up from their reading with an air of utter disbelief that the audience is laughing, thereby adding to the fun of the audience. In reading, pauses are quite as important as filling the air with words.

Therefore, it is not a bad idea to read material carefully, first to yourself and then perhaps to a sympathetic listener or two. This should help you later to read more naturally before a larger group.

Preparing for the Unexpected. Many of the skits and some of the stories, boners, and the like in this collection can be used on the spur of the moment. The wise leader will have a few "spares" ready, either on a card, on which page numbers of the book to be used are noted, or on separate cards with directions written out and the cards arranged alphabetically by title of game for quick reference.

Here is an illustration of how one leader provided recreation on the spur of the moment. In a conference of eighteen hundred high school and college youth a fun period was inserted unexpectedly, to last a forty-five minute stretch in the auditorium. What to do? Group singing answered part of the problem; and then the reading of about twenty boners, slowly and giving time for laughs, brought much fun to the group. The crowd also played Fox, Hunter, and Gun with the leader. Afterward some of the men and women leaders did it as a group activity on the stage, to the amusement of the audience. The fortune-telling or dream analysis sort of stunt fitted in here (see "Group Fortune Telling" in *Handy Stunts*) and several other group participation stunts. The time went fast for both leadership and group.

Taking a Theme. In a camp, conference, or school where the group has common life all day long for several days, it is often customary to take a theme for an entire day. Some of the themes are reasonably serious in nature, but some by their very title indicate fun, such as these: "The Circus Comes Tonight," with all-day preparation for it; or "Gridiron Gambol," a football party "under the lights," with sides chosen, cheers given, parades, and bonfires (see *The End of Your Stunt Hunt* for a complete description).

A Day in the Life of Ma and Pa Settle

One 4-H camp group took as its theme "A Day in the Life of Ma and Pa Settle" and worked toward it all day. Here is a report of their experience, to give you ideas.[4]

SADIE HAWKINS RACE

This group did many of the usual "mountain" tricks, and added some twists of their own. For the Sadie Hawkins race, the girls as well as the boys had a chance to exercise and practice up. Marryin' Sam gave "spiels" about his bargains in weddin's." (The boys finally threw him into the lake.) They were about to have the race when a boy came in ex-

[4] From Mrs. R. O. Bechtel, Wakarusha, Ind.

citedly with a calendar and indicated that it was two days too late! (Here the starter could either accept his statement or rule him out of order and go ahead with the race.) The girl catching a boy had him for a partner in activities for the rest of the day.

HILLBILLY HOT ROD

There was the Hillbilly Hot Rod. This was a variation on the old automobile stunt, in which the players bend over and catch their ankles to form tires, one person in the front with hand stuck out as the motor to be cranked. The body is formed with chairs. These folk were on their way to the city.

FIRE!

Another group's stunt was the burning of the "Abe Martin," announced excitedly, as people came running with cupfuls of water. Or was it water? "No, it's kerosene," was the punch line.

CUT OFF MY WIND

Still another group had a stunt in which Ma calls the family to supper. As they eat noisily they miss Pa and go out to the barn, where they find him trying to hang himself with a rope around his waist. "Why didn't you put it around your neck?" he is asked. "'Cause it cut off my wind," is Pa's answer.

DAISY MAE

During the entire evening one of the older girls walked around through the audience or on the stage, carrying a basket and a baby, and eating and "chomping" on mud mushrooms. She would come up to the master of ceremonies and stand gazing at him and chewing incessantly. He would ask for some mushrooms, but she would refuse because they were "habit formin'." Then she would rush away for more. She kept getting heavier and heavier. Near the end she gave the "MC" a bite, and both rushed offstage for more mushrooms. When the "MC" appeared the last time he was eating them ravenously and was noticeably fatter.

SEWING MACHINE TRIO

For music, one group used the "Sewing Machine Trio" gag—"not a singer in the bunch!"

WRESTLING

One boy well over six feet tall wrestled with a youngster under five feet. The short boy always won the falls.

With a theme idea, it is necessary to have a central committee (if stunts are to be planned by different groups) to tie the stunts together and to avoid duplication. It is wise to have one person head the entire enterprise; often that person acts as the Master of Ceremonies.

WHERE TO FIND SKIT AND STUNT IDEAS

Of course, in the public library, there are many books on recreation which contain skits and stunts. One of the uses of a prepared collection like this one is to give people an idea of the forms that skits and stunts may take. This book presents a considerable variety of ways of having fun with skits, stunts, and stories. With these *form* ideas in mind, many clever planning committees and groups can adapt them very well to local situations, thus giving the skits added interest.

Ideas can be gleaned from many sources—for instance, from the jokes that we read and hear on every hand. The comics—both the four-or-five picture kind of the comic strips, and the one-picture cartoons—have ideas for sketches and humorous tableau presentation. Many television and radio programs, particularly those of the "comics," are right along the skit-stunt line. Radio quiz shows, television soap operas, movie serials—all these may be full of suggestions for skits and stunts. So, too, are scenes from daily life: like the policeman with traffic trouble, the thief who opens a safe and finds only a gallon of glue in it; the man doing shopping for his wife.

The Eternal Charade

When thinking of skits and stunts one must always include charades as a possibility. The typical situation is to divide a large group into small ones and let each group pick a word to dramatize, usually one syllable at a time. Many variations on charades have been worked out. Here are two:

1. *Charades as a group game.* Divide into two sides, each having a captain. All members of both teams jot down the hardest word to act that occurs to them. The captains gather up the slips of their own groups. The leader gets a slip from one captain, shows it to that captain's entire team, and then it is assigned to one person on the opposite side for dramatizing. While he is being timed in minutes and seconds, he must pantomime the word for his team. Some groups use an elaborate signal system, but it is really better sport to use a simple one. His team may ask questions that must be answered "yes" or "no" (he indicates by nodding or shaking his head). He may hold up fingers to indicate the number of syllables or to show which syllable he is acting out. The object, of course, is to have the lowest use of elapsed time. The teams alternate in this procedure.

This is a good game for an audience to watch, with a small group on the stage or in some other spot visible from the audience. In this case, the audience, as well as the first team, knows the word the actor is trying to dramatize.

2. *One-person charades.* Sometimes one person acts out a word for an entire group. Some illustrations of words often used for charades are these: hand-cur-chief, buck-can-ear, saw-sage, in-fan-sea, ought-toe-mow-bill, melon-collie, press-bee-teary-Ann. Many groups go further into names of trees,

birds, flowers, famous people; or scenes from the Bible, Shakespeare, Mother Goose; or titles of songs or books.

Doodles and Droodles

There is a type of stunt that is suggested by drawing pictures on the blackboard. Doodles may be done on a blackboard by several players before the entire group. Someone starts with the chalk, drawing a semicircle, a straight line, and a wiggly line, all connected. Then anyone in the group who has an idea of how this may be completed into a picture comes forward to do it. (The picture may be a person, an object, or a scene.) The newer fad, "Droodles," involves drawing some object and then giving a tricky interpretation to the object drawn, for instance, a perpendicular line with fuzzy marks on each end: "mop for cleaning floor and ceiling at the same time." Members of the group enjoy sharing such "information" if they have it, and creating others.

Horror Song Titles

One group has great fun perverting the titles of all the currently popular songs, such as "Singing in the Drain," and "With a Prong in My Heart."[5] Within the fellowship of a group, particularly a youth group, this kind of nonsense and its enjoyment develop spontaneously.

[5] Bill Wilson, Vanderbilt University, Nashville, Tenn.

chapter 2

STUNTS

AND

STORIES

LET'S TRY 'EM

stunts for the leader alone
stunts for leader and group
stories told by the leader
when the group joins in the story

STUNTS AND STORIES?
LET'S TRY 'EM

T HE LEADER of social fun often finds that he must take the initiative in bringing enjoyment to the group or audience—sometimes as a solo performer. This chapter is intended to provide him with material for such situations.

Many of the stunts, tricks, and narratives here may be done readily by one person. A few of them will require assistance by one or two partners. Other stunts and stories included in this section are to be done by leader and audience together—the leader reading the narrative and the audience acting out what is read.

Among the most useful items are those which can be read to groups—boners and short, punchy stories in the Spoonerism form of Colonel Stoopnagle, and in the "Pennsylvania Dutch" form of Dave Morrah.

A few of the stunts involve playing a trick on someone. Though it has a place, this sort of stunt should be used sparingly and carefully. To embarrass someone, especially about a physical handicap, represents neither good taste, kindliness, nor group sensitivity. If you are in doubt as to whether a certain trick or stunt will be hurtful or embarrassing, try some other type of entertainment. This book is loaded with suggestions, and no one need use any kind of entertainment that is not in good taste.

STUNTS FOR THE LEADER ALONE
How to Make Money Fast

In a club or other organization, this topic could be widely advertised as a subject to be dealt with at the next meeting. A fabulous leader such as "Andrew Carnegie" or "Hetty

Green" might be announced as the one presenting the subject.

When the leader actually takes up the topic, he smears some glue on a coin, and lays the coin, glue side down, on an old table, piece of glass, or other object. He then points out that of all the ways he knows, that is the best way to make money fast.

Where to Find Sympathy[1]

No matter where you are, what you've done, how much trouble you've been in, you can always find sympathy. Yes, you can find it if you will look up Richard Shonáry. You don't know Richard Shonáry? Well, maybe you know him better as Dick Shonáry.

The Disjointed Finger

Bend the knuckle of the left index finger; place the bent knuckle against the bent knuckle of the right thumb. Cover the joints with the right index finger, then pull away with the right hand.

Baby's Cradle

Here is mamma's knife and fork,	*(With fingers interlaced, hold palms up.)*
Here is mamma's table.	*(With fingers joined, turn hands over.)*
Here is sister's looking glass,	*(Raise index fingers.)*
And here is baby's cradle.	*(Raise little fingers, and rock.)*

The Rubber Arm

To do this effectively you need to be wearing a coat or shirt with loose sleeves. Work the cuff down over the hand in advance. Then, by pulling on the end of the hand or wrist

[1] From Eber Bowles, Huntington, W. Va.

and at the same time straightening the arm, the illusion of stretching the arm is given.

Two Crooks

Bend your elbow and place two bent fingers under the elbow joint. What does this represent? "A couple of crooks holding up a joint."

Nonsense Speech[2]

Last night yesterday morning, late in the afternoon about one o'clock, a young man about forty years old bought a pudding for a brick, threw it through a stone wall nine feet thick, jumped over it and broke his left knee on the right leg just below the ankle, fell into a dry millpond and drowned.

About forty years later on the same day an old tomcat had nine turkey gobblers while a strong east wind blew Yankee Doodle onto a frying pan, killed a hog and two dead pigs way down in Boston where a deaf and dumb man stood talking to his Aunt Pete.

(The person who contributed this nonsense patter says that her father taught it to her when she was three years old!)

Who Is So Smart?

Once there were two worms. One was energetic, got up early in the mornings, and went about his business. The other one was lazy, stayed out late, and always got up late. Well, the early bird got the early worm, and a fisherman with a flashlight got the night crawler. Moral: You can't win.

Peter Rabbit

The storyteller accompanies this story with appropriate motions. He makes a hand motion to indicate the rabbit's

[2] From Tillie Bruce, Goshen, Ind.

rush every day and his rush to the meadow. He shows a grab as Peter Rabbit catches a field mouse, then he makes the motions of bashing the mouse with his fist and eating it up. The motions are repeated, of course, each time the descriptions of the actions are repeated.

THE STORY

Peter Rabbit was having the time of his life.

Every day he would rush from the thicket, rush to the meadow, catch a field mouse, bash out his brains, and eat him all up.

One day his fairy godmother said to him, "Peter Rabbit, you must not rush from the thicket, rush to the meadow, catch a field mouse, bash out his brains, and eat him all up, or I'll make you into a G-unk." (This sound is made in the throat.)

But in a day or two Peter Rabbit couldn't resist, so he rushed from the thicket, rushed to the meadow, caught a field mouse, bashed out his brains, and ate him all up.

And his fairy godmother found out about it—and immediately changed him into a G-unk!

The moral of this story is: Hare today—G-unk tomorrow!

What the Clock Says

TEACHER: Jimmie, if the big hand of the clock is at the eight and the little hand is at the three, what does the clock say?

JIMMIE: Tick-tock!

Modern Efficiency[3]

This stunt has been done in various forms ever since Henry Ford first developed the assembly line. The actions vary a little, and the punch line somewhat. It is often done as a monologue, the speaker acting both parts.

[3] From Doris Curtis, Arkansaw, Wis.

SCENE I

HENRY FORD: Good morning, Pat.

PAT: Mornin', Mr. Ford.

FORD: What about working on my assembly line?

PAT: Sure, an' I'd be glad to.

FORD: Well, all you have to do is to turn this knob right here with your right hand, and you'll get five dollars a day for that.

PAT: Fine. (*He turns the knob.*) Now I'll make lots of money and keep my wife and kids happy. (*Keeps turning and turning the knob.*)

SCENE II

Pat comes in and starts turning his knob when Ford walks in.

HENRY FORD: Good morning, Pat.

PAT: Mornin', Mr. Ford.

FORD: How are you coming?

PAT: Fine.

FORD: Well, we've been making a time and motion study, and we believe it would help us for you to turn this knob over with your left hand at the same time. I'll raise your pay one dollar a day.

PAT: Fine. (*Turns one knob with right hand, another with left.*) Now I'll have more money to keep my wife and kids happy! (*Keeps turning both knobs.*)

SCENE III

Pat comes to work, starts turning his two knobs when Ford walks in.

FORD: Good morning, Pat.

PAT: Mornin', Mr. Ford.

FORD: How are you getting along?

PAT: Fine. (*Still turns both knobs.*)

FORD: We've made another time and motion study, and we

believe you could push a lever with your left foot while you're doing your other work.

PAT: Well, I'll try. (*He turns one knob, turns the other knob, pushes out his left foot as if kicking a lever.*)

FORD: I'll raise your pay one dollar a week if you'll do that.

PAT: It's a deal, Mr. Ford. (*Continues to do these three motions.*)

SCENE IV

Pat comes to work, starts doing his three operations.

FORD: Good morning, Pat.

PAT: Mornin', Mr. Ford.

FORD: How are you getting along?

PAT: Fine, fine.

FORD: We've been making a time and motion study again, and we believe you can push this lever with your right foot, as well as doing the other things, without hurting your efficiency.

PAT: Well, I'll try. (*Continues with first three motions, adds kicking forward with right foot.*)

FORD: I'll raise your pay one dollar a week if you'll do that.

PAT: Fine, Mr. Ford. Now I'll have more money to keep my wife and kids happy.

SCENE V

Pat comes to work, does his four operations.

FORD: Good morning, Pat.

PAT: Mornin', Mr. Ford.

FORD: How are you getting along?

PAT: Fine.

FORD: We've been making a time and motion study, and we believe you can close the doors of the cars coming down the line in addition to your other jobs—like this. (*Ford shows him how to close the left door with a flip of the left hip, the right door with a flip of the right hip.*)

PAT: Well, I'll try. *(Does his first four operations, adds this one.)*

FORD: That's fine. I'll give you two dollars more a day for doing this.

PAT: Fine, Mr. Ford. Now I'll have more money to keep my wife and kiddies happy.

SCENE VI

Pat comes to work and is doing all his operations.

FORD: Good morning, Pat.

PAT: Mornin', Mr. Ford. *(Continues his operations.)*

FORD: How are you getting along?

PAT: Fine, Mr. Ford. Now *I* have a suggestion. *(Continues operations.)*

FORD: All right, what is it, Pat?

PAT: If you'll just get me a long grass skirt and tie it around my waist, I'll sweep the floor for you and not charge you a cent!

STUNTS FOR LEADER AND GROUP

The first ten stunts which follow are for the leader and an assistant.

Feel the Pain

The leader has a "volunteer" who is going around the room, touching the wall. "Do you feel it?" the leader asks. "No," replies the volunteer. Repeatedly the leader asks, and gets the same answer. The volunteer comes to the window. "Do you feel it now?" "Yes," says the volunteer. (Perhaps he howls suddenly to make this more dramatic.) "What did you feel?" "I felt the pane."

Wrap at the Door[4]

One person says, "Say, wasn't there a rap at the door?" Another says, "Why, no, I don't think so."

[4] From Tillie Bruce, Goshen, Ind.

"Yes, I think there was a rap at the door!"

"I don't think so."

The first one then goes to the door and brings in a coat, saying, "I was just sure there was a wrap at the door."

She's Lovely

During a beauty show, or as an individual stunt, have a girl walk acrosss the stage while you remark about her, "She's lovely. . . . She's engaged. . . . She uses Jiu-jitsu." (A man dressed as a girl would be even funnier, of course.)

Remove the Dime[5]

In view of all the audience, have a person lie flat on the floor and place a dime on his nose. He is to get it off without moving his head if he can. He can't (unless he reaches up and removes it).

Pinning the Tin Cup[6]

Did you know that you can pin a tin cup to the wall? Well, come over here and help! (As the initiator is trying to pin the cup to the wall he accidentally [on purpose] drops the pin, and asks the assistant to pick it up. The assistant then gets some water spilled on him from the cup, accidentally!)

That's Your Sentence

Get two talkative persons, perhaps leaders, before the group. They are to take the sentences assigned to them, such as "What is the price of eggs in China?" and "Did Peter Piper pick a peck of pickled peppers?" Neither one knows what the other's sentence is, but the audience knows.

Each of these persons is trying to get his sentence said first before the other one can say, "That's your sentence." If

[5] From Paul Weaver, Elgin, Ill.

[6] *Ibid.*

the challenge is successful, the challenger wins. If a speaker, however, says his sentence unchallenged and goes beyond it in speech, he is the winner.

They swap sentences, one at a time, each one working cautiously to bring the conversation around to the point at which he can slip in his sentence unnoticed. A sample of the first few sentences might be:

EGGS: You know, Bill, inflation has hit the people in China.

PIPER: Yes, but in this country the labor situation is our problem.

EGGS: Right, but we still don't have to pay so much for things as they do in the East.

PIPER: Yes, but the labor is so inefficient that they can't do what they used to do.

Here you can see that "Eggs" is trying to slip in his sentence, using the inflation angle, while "Piper" is going to ask if his opponent really believes that Peter Piper picked a peck of pickled peppers. This is good both as a stunt and as a sort of contest.

Making Three Squares

"I believe I can make three squares with three pencils. Don't remember for sure," one person says. Then he tries a while. "If I'm in the wrong will you buy me a milkshake?" Usually the person challenged will say, "Yes." "I'm wrong," the first person says!

BAIK

In a conference or meeting in which many figures have been given, and ideas thrown out freely, this stunt is particularly appropriate. A person comes in, wearing a big "button" with letters large enough for all to see: "BAIK."

"Say, what is that?" someone asks him.

"My club badge."

"What club?"

"The BAIK Club."

"What does that stand for?"

"Brother, Am I Konfused."

"But you don't spell 'confused' with a K."

"Brother, that proves how confused I am!"

Spot Announcement

"We interrupt this program to bring you a very important spot announcement."

"Arf, arf," says the stooge.

"Thank you, Spot."

Mind Reading

The "mind reader" with magic powers is introduced to the group. He can tell the owner of any object just by holding it in his hand. (He does not point out of course that he has a confederate.)

The mind reader leaves the room, and when he returns he is given an object furnished by the person selected. His confederate handing it to him, says, "Knock down the answer, Professor." He immediately guesses "Kay Davis" from the initials of the first two words.

The whole audience will co-operate with the leader in the stunts which follow.

What You'll Say![7]

This is really not a gag, but an experiment in group response. The leader writes down in advance the answers that the people will give, handing the slip to someone in the audience who will read it aloud after the finish.

Then he calls on all to respond immediately when he gives the cue. He will say, "One, two, three . . . ," give the category under which he wants them to name something

[7] From E. L. Crump, Aum-Sat-Tat Ranch, Texas.

specific, and then clap his hands. All are supposed to say aloud the answer that first occurs to them.

For a sample run, the leader takes this: "One, two, three . . . a numeral." Then in the same rhythm he claps his hands together, and immediately the group must respond. There will probably be some variation with that category, but it will be interesting to see how many will respond to these class nouns with the same answer:

1. "A color"—red.
2. "An article of furniture"—chair.
3. "Something to eat"—bread.
4. "A flower"—rose.
5. "Girl's name"—Mary.

Not every person in a group will respond identically, but in most groups most people will give these answers. You might experiment with other categories. By way of illustration: "A popular sport," "A boy's name," "A tree," "Something to drink," "A metal," "The name of a city," "A profession," "A berry," "A vegetable." Audiences are amazed, yet the similarity of response is not a trick.

Count to Thirty

Get eight or ten boys or men and eight or ten girls or women up in front of the group to "count to thirty." First the girls start, giving aloud a number, beginning with "one," and going from left to right (or starting wherever the leader points). The rule is that they must, instead of saying a numeral with a "seven" in it put palms together, and on a number divisible by seven, put hands together back to back (knuckles of center fingers touching). All other numbers are called aloud. Further rule: when one of these symbols has been given, the counting reverses in direction and goes down the line the opposite way. It is very hard to count to thirty. (Have boys cheer for boys, girls for girls.)

Matching Fingers

The leader holds a hand aloft and as he brings it forward toward the group holds up as many or as few fingers as he wishes. It is fun to see how many can match fingers with him out of ten or twenty tries.

Button Up Your Coat

This stunt is usable only when men are wearing coats. Ask the men to unbutton their coats and button them up again. See how many can follow instructions. (Most men button coats from the top *down,* not from the bottom *up.*)

This could also be used as a performance stunt, by having leaders or other persons come to the front to see if they can follow instructions.

Fox-Hunter-Gun

This may be played as a *party game,* as an audience *warm-upper,* or as a wonderful *performance stunt,* with slight variations in its use.

The fox wins over (or is superior to) the hunter because it can outrun him.

The hunter wins over the gun because he can control it.

The gun wins over the fox because it can kill the fox.

The fox is represented by the player's putting his thumbs in both his ears and waggling the fingers.

The gun is indicated by pointing the forefingers of each hand, the left hand behind the right.

The hunter (or "man") is represented by folded arms.

As a *party game,* the one who is It goes around a circle of people and in front of each person, in turn, he takes the part of either fox, hunter, or gun. Before It counts to ten, the person he faces must represent by his posture the superior one or become It. For example, if It has extended his forefingers (taken the part of the gun), the person It is facing must quickly fold his arms or become It.

As a group stunt for a *warm-upper,* each person in the group faces one other person. On the count of "One, two, three—GO!" each one represents toward his opponent what he hopes is the superior one. If he wins, he gets a point. (This may also be played in threes.)

As a *performance stunt,* several of the men and women leaders of the group are asked to come forward (or to the platform). This may be after the entire group has played it in the manner of the "warm-upper" above. It is explained that there will be a huddle for the men and one for the women. Each huddle is to decide on one symbol. When ready, they line up facing the other sex. When both lines are in place, the leader once again gives out, "One, two, three—GO!" and on the Go signal the entire line, simultaneously, represents the symbol of its choice. When the men or boys who are not participating directly yell for their sex and the women or girls cheer for theirs, the game can be quite exciting. It is played for five to nine tries. There may be ties, which, of course, do not count.

Dead Finger

Put the palm of your right hand against your partner's left palm, with index fingers against each other. Now take your free hand and press with thumb and finger of the free hand the two index fingers. Fingers feel "dead" on stroking.

Elephant

Several persons are brought before the group in a line, either standing or sitting. The leader explains that when he points to a person, that person must form an elephant's trunk with his two fists, one on his nose and the other below it. At the same time, the person at his left must form an elephant ear by cupping his hand and placing it on the "elephant's" ear. The person on the right forms the right ear. The last one finishing his job (of the three) becomes It. The situation is more humorous if leaders are drawn into the stunt.

Band Players[8]

This is a group or audience participation stunt. Give each person a rubber band and let him or her play a tune by stretching the band tight and plucking it. The stunt could be used in several ways, with one person coming forward and playing while all listen, or by having each person in the group play a tune for one other person (as at a banquet).

Glass or Bottle Players

This is the same idea as Band Players, but instead running the finger lightly around the rim of a glass of water—each tumbler containing a different level of water. Or bottles can be filled to different levels of water and tapped with a silver knife.

Bubble Dance[9]

One person, or a group, comes out with large balloons. Someone announces with a flourish that a great Bubble Dance is to be presented. Then he produces a magic bubble bottle and makes bubbles while dancing about in front of the others. (Piano or recorded music is used.) Participants might be called up from the audience for the first part and be handed their balloons—or better, taken out and coached for the Bubble Dance.

Opposites[10]

This stunt is used just to encourage an audience to respond quickly. The leader points to his knee and says, "This is my face," and counts quickly to ten. Each person is supposed to

[8] From Tillie Bruce, Goshen, Ind.
[9] *Ibid.*
[10] From James Perry, Zirconia, N. C.

touch his own face and say, "This is my knee." Each person keeps his own score.

Glass Forfeit[11]

Supply each table or group with an empty glass or container. When the music starts, or at the signal "Go," the glasses are passed rapidly around the table. When the music stops, whoever has the glass puts in a penny. The music starts several times and stops; each time a forfeit is named —one cent, five cents, ten cents. There are several variations —such as occasionally allowing people to take out a coin instead of dropping one in. Also, it is fun to catch someone not putting his coin in and to hold a trial or a censure of some sort.

Napkin Bite[12]

Ask everyone in the room to take his napkin in hand and to make numerous folds as instructed by you. Fold your own napkin slowly so that all can follow. Each napkin gets thicker and thicker. Tell the group that it is important to have a good crease here at this fold, and ask everyone to put his napkin in his mouth and bite on it firmly. At this point you announce that the demonstration is over—that you needed to see how many would bite on it!

Rhythmic Spelling[13]

This novel stunt is very interesting to audiences. It may be used in several ways:

1. Ask several persons, especially officers or leaders, to come to the front and spell words given them according to the rules given below.
2. For a "warm-upper" of a group, the leader gives out

11 From Paul Weaver, Elgin, Ill.
12 *Ibid.*
13 From Leona Holbrook, Provo, Utah.

words—and the entire audience stands and tries to spell them out.

3. This is carried out as in No. 2, except that the audience is divided into partners (your partner being the person closest to you). Partner No. 1 spells for No. 2, and vice versa.

RULES: To spell the word, you jump together on both feet for the consonants and on the left foot only for vowels. Variation: Use alternate feet for the vowels. Certain words give pleasant rhythms. Experiment!

Candy Under Hat

Having three hats and a piece of candy in evidence, send someone as It out of the room, or out of hearing. Explain to the group that you are going to ask It to guess which hat the candy is under. Get the audience to select the hat under which they want the candy placed. Then you say, "Fine," and, putting the hat on your head, you eat the candy!

Stick Out Tongue, Touch Nose

Ask the group if they can stick out their tongues and touch their noses. After several tries on their part, show them how: simply stick out your tongue and touch your nose with your finger.

Qt, Mt

Each of these stunts is done with partners. (At the table or in a crowded space, your partner may be the person next to you.) One partner is to put his forefinger under the chin of his partner and say three times the abbreviation for "quart." For the other stunt the same idea is used, but the abbreviation for "mountain" is asked for, and this time he is to pat his partner on the head three times.

Can You Poke a Quarter Through a Ring?

This question is asked, and several tries may be made by members of the group. Of course it isn't hard if you "poke it" with a pencil or like object through the ring!

Rabbit

This is an older stunt, but some have not seen it and get great fun from it. One person kneels on the floor and asks several others to join him in playing "Rabbit." They kneel on the floor in a circle. The leader asks the others, one at a time, if they know how to play Rabbit. The answer is, of course, "No." "Well, then, what are we doing down here on the floor?" he asks after a while.

Proving That a Person Is Not Here[14]

The leader tells the group he can prove that a person in the group is really not here—by talking with that person! He calls him up to the front or gets him into a place for a good conversation.

"Are you in New York?"

"No," the person will reply.

"Are you in Dallas?"

"No."

"Are you in Seattle?"

"No."

"Well, if you are not in New York, or Dallas, or Seattle, you must be someplace else. Right?"

"Yes."

"And if you are someplace else, you just can't be here!"

How to Pronounce It

How do you pronounce the name of the capital of Kentucky—"Louis-ville," or "Louee-ville"? This question is asked

[14] From Paul Weaver, Elgin, Ill.

of the group or of an individual. (If the group is asked, have them hold up their hands for their choice.) Then say, "No, that's not quite right. The capital of Kentucky is pronounced 'Frankfort.'"

The Name of Your Future Wife

"How many of the men in this audience are married?" (Get them to hold up their hands.)

"How many of the women, now?"

"How many of the women are not married?"

"How many men?"

"We have with us tonight a person who can tell you the name of your future mate. Here he is—Dr. Follett." (Dr. Follett comes out.) "First, let's take one of the young men. Will someone hold up his hand?"

"What is your name?" (He replies, "Bill Harbin.") Dr. Follett ponders for a minute.

"I have it," says Dr. Follett. "The name of your future wife will be . . . Mrs. Harbin."

Reach Behind You

"Let's have some friendly spirit here," says the leader. "Everybody shake hands with the person on your right. (All do so.) Now turn in the other direction and shake hands with that person. Get acquainted with him. (Give them time.) Now, on a signal, I want you all to do with me at the same time what I say. Now, turn around and SHAKE HANDS WITH THE PERSON BEHIND YOU!" (If all turn around, then there is no "person behind," for that person is turned around, too!)

Telling Right from Left

"How many of you folks here have difficulty sometimes telling your right from your left?" (Probably almost all will indicate that they do.) "Well, here's a sure help. Will you raise your right hand?" (Wait for them to do so.) "I want you to note that your thumb is pointing toward your left."

Ducks Fly

When the leader calls out that a certain animal does something which it actually does, the group responds. "Ducks fly" calls for all to make flying motions. "Donkeys bray"— and they all do it. But if the leader calls out, "Donkeys neigh," of course the group does not neigh. The leader imitates the sound immediately after he has announced it. Many will join in who are not supposed to, of course, and that is part of the fun.

Your Dream Interpreted

Some folks believe in dream interpretations and some do not, but all can have fun with these interpretations. They can be used in several ways:

1. They can be given by someone who is dressed in mystic fashion and who sits in a booth at a carnival or circus. He carefully checks with the "clients," interpreting their dreams (by asking them if they have ever dreamed of these objects).

2. A leader of a group, master of ceremonies, or toastmaster may use these interpretations by asking the group if they have ever dreamed of, say, a balloon. Then, after a show of hands he gives them the interpretation.

3. Audience participation can be secured by writing the items below on slips of paper in advance, and by having the leader point out that he has a number of assistants in the audience to interpret dreams. Then, for example, he may ask the group if they have ever dreamed of "hot water." How many ever have? (In order to make sure that he has some "takers," he may have some stooges in the audience who have dreamed his whole list!) Then he says, "We have a student of dream interpretation who can give us the signifi-

cance." The person having the slip rises and reads or says, "If you dream of hot water, be nonchalant—take a bath." This is continued for as many of the dream interpretations as have been passed out on slips in the group. This is an effective manner for bringing the participation of some who would not otherwise be active in a stunt.

Be sure to add others as you think of them. This listing is only illustrative of possibilities. This is supposed to be nonsense, of course.

If you dream of (a or an)—

1. Balloon . . . you are going up in the world.
2. Automobile . . . you may become very poor.
3. New clothes . . . a change is coming in your life.
4. Camera . . . life is going to be a snap from now on.
5. Acorn . . . next time you take off your shoes, look carefully.
6. Goat . . . be careful. You may become the butt of some trick.
7. Altar . . . you need to alter your ways. (If unmarried, you may need to alter your appearance.)
8. Bear . . . look out—somebody is going to hug you.
9. Romantic novel . . . have a care! You are reading things into life that are not there.
10. Camel . . . have courage—you will soon be over the hump.
11. Buttermilk . . . life may be sour for a while.
12. Chestnuts . . . caution! Look out! You may get roasted.
13. Canary . . . this calls for caution. Do not give your friends the bird.
14. Hot water . . . Be nonchalant. Take a bath.
15. Explosion . . . Be careful that things don't blow up in your face.

16. Animals . . . you are leading a dog's life.
17. Birds . . . be careful when walking under trees.
18. Fan . . . it's a warning that you are a big blow and should be quiet.
19. Fog . . . a political campaign is coming soon.
20. Lake . . . take it easy. Your friends may want you to go jump in.
21. Wheat . . . it's a good sign, but don't get puffed up about it.
22. Satan . . . somebody resents you because you are trying to horn in. (It may be that you are expected to fork over.)
23. Shot . . . take delight—your ideas are going over with a bang.
24. Snow . . . you must explain your ideas more simply. People do not get your drift.
25. Violin . . . stop fiddling around and get to work.
26. Zebra, if accompanied by stars . . . this gives you a combination of stars and stripes, indicating that you will get a government job.
27. Clam . . . if you want to stay out of trouble, keep your mouth shut.

A Christmas Story[15]

Have the group answer the following questions on a numbered sheet of paper. Then read slowly "A Visit from St. Nicholas," by Clement Clarke Moore, and let them see how their answers fit into the story. *Do not tell them what the story is to be* until they have written the answers. Get them to write fast.

It might be good to have each person exchange papers with his neighbor, just to make the fun a little more social; or, if the group are seated in a circle, have one at a time, in

15 From Mary Lib McDonald, Birmingham, Ala.

succession, call out what he has written for the correspond-
ing blank, as the reader pauses. Give time for the funny ones
to be shared with all as they are being read.

Fill in the blanks

1. Time of day _____
2. A holiday _____
3. A building _____
4. An animal _____
5. Wearing apparel _____
6. Famous charac-
   ter _____
7. Relaxed _____
8. Good to eat _____
9. Part of the body _____
10. Married woman _____
11. Wearing apparel _____
12. Quick action _____
13. Article of furni-
    ture _____
14. Shines in the
    sky _____
15. Part of the body _____
16. Child's toy _____
17. Animals _____
18. In good spirits _____
19. Fast _____
20. Famous charac-
    ter _____
21. Large bird _____
22. Eight first names of
    people you know _____

23. Part of a house _____
24. Part of a yard _____
25. Part of a build-
    ing _____
26. Sweetmeats _____
27. Like a star _____
28. Part of the body _____
29. World-famous per-
    son _____
30. Quality coat ma-
    terial _____
31. Holes in the face _____
32. Favorite flowers _____
33. Favorite fruit _____
34. A color _____
35. Decoration _____
36. Upper part of
    body_____
37. Roundfaced _____
38. Round in front _____
39. Upper part of
    body _____
40. Vigorous body
    action _____
41. Child's toy _____
42. Friendly greeting_____

And here is the Christmas story:

'Twas the . . . (1) . . . before . . . (2) . . . when all through the
    . . . (3) . . .,
Not a creature was stirring—not even a . . . (4). . . .

The . . . (5) . . . were hung by the chimney with care,
In hopes that . . . (6) . . . soon would be there.
The children were . . . (7) . . ., all snug in their beds,
While visions of . . . (8) . . . danced in their . . . (9) . . .,
And . . . (10) . . in her kerchief, and I in my . . . (11). . . .
Had just settled down for a long winter's nap,
When out on the lawn there rose such a clatter,
I . . . (12) . . . from my . . . (13) . . . to see what was the
   matter.

Away to the window I flew like a flash,
Tore open the shutter and threw up the sash.
The . . . (14) . . . on the breast of the new-fallen snow
Gave a luster of midday to objects below.
When what to my wondering . . . (15) . . . should appear
But a miniature . . . (16) . . . and eight tiny . . . (17) . . .!
With a little old driver so . . . (18) . . . and . . . (19) . . .,
I knew in a moment it must be . . . (20). . . .
More rapid than . . . (21) . . ., his coursers they came,
And he whistled and shouted, and called them by name:

"Now, . . . (22) . . ., now, . . . (22) . . ., now, . . . (22) . . .,
   now, . . . (22) . . .,
On, . . . (22) . . ., on, . . . (22) . . ., on, . . . (22) . . ., and
   . . . (22) . . .!
To the top of the . . . (23) . . ., to the top of the . . . (24) . . .,
Now dash away, dash away, dash away, all!"
So up to the . . . (25) . . . the coursers, they flew,
With a bag full of toys and . . . (26) . . ., too.

And then in . . . (27) . . . I heard on the roof,
The prancing and pawing of each little hoof.
As I drew in my . . . (28) . . . and was turning around,
Down the chimney . . . (29) . . . came with a bound.
He was dressed all in . . . (30) . . . from his head to his foot,
And his clothes were all tarnished with ashes and soot.

A bundle of toys he had flung on his back
And he looked like a peddler just opening his pack.

His eyes, how they twinkled, his . . . (31) . . . how merry,
His cheeks were like . . . (32) . . ., his nose like a . . . (33) . . .,
His droll little mouth was drawn up like a bow,
And the beard on his chin was as . . (34) . . . as the snow.
The stump of a pipe he held tight in his teeth,
And the smoke it encircled his head like a . . . (35). . . .

He had a broad . . . (3) . . . , and a round little belly,
That shook when he laughed like a bowl full of jelly.
He was . . . (37) . . . and . . . (38) . . ., a right jolly old elf,
And I laughed when I saw him in spite of myself.

A wink of his eye and a twist of his . . . (39) . . .
Soon gave me to know I had nothing to dread.
He spoke not a word, but went straight to his work;
And filled all the stockings, then turned with a jerk.
And he laid his finger aside of his nose,
And giving a nod, up the chimney he rose.
He . . . (40) . . . to his . . . (41) . . . , to his team gave a
    whistle,
And away they all flew like the down of a thistle.
But we heard him exclaim ere he drove out of sight,
"Merry Christmas to all, and to all a . . . (42) . . . .

Boners[16]

Since the first collection of these schoolboy howlers was
published in the late twenties, they have been delighting
all who have ever been to school and made similar mistakes.

We have included a large number of them here, with several uses in mind:

16 From *Bigger and Better Boners* and *Boner Books*. Copyright 1931, 1932,
1951, and 1952 by The Viking Press, Inc. Reprinted by permission of The
Viking Press, Inc., New York. Cartoons from *Pocketbook of Boners* also by
courtesy of The Viking Press, Inc.

1. Simply to read to a group, small or large, for fun.
2. As "raw material" for making up a School Days stunt, with various "pupils" answering the "teacher's" questions. This is illustrated below.
3. To pass the boners out on numbered slips to the audience. Call for them by number. If the group know one another well it might be more fun to call the individuals by name, their boners to be read aloud by them to all.
4. To indicate that the group or club has recently had an intelligence test. Then read some of the "answers," and attribute them to certain members of the group.
5. To be read, just for fun, to yourself or a friend. (*Bigger and Better Boners*, Viking Press, will give you many more.)

SCHOOL DAZE

This skit is given as an illustration of the use of "boners" in the classroom. An entire evening might be given over to a "School Daze" theme with performances, musical stunts, and the like, and with the use of boners at the recitation period.

PROFESSOR: Good morning, children.

CHILDREN *(together):* Good morning, teacher!

PROFESSOR: Have you studied your lessons yet? Did you write your papers?

CHILDREN *(in chorus):* Yes, teacher.

PROFESSOR: Well, well, we shall see. Roberta, who was Queen Victoria?

ROBERTA *(proudly reading):* Queen Victoria was the only queen who sat on a thorn for sixty-three years.

PROFESSOR: That's odd. Billy, what is chivalry?

BILLY: Chivalry is the attitude of a man toward a strange woman.

PROFESSOR: There's truth in that statement, boy. Sam, what is an eavesdropper?

SAM: An eavesdropper is a sort of bird, I think.

PROFESSOR: Mary Jane, what is a skeleton?

MARY JANE: A skeleton is . . . a skeleton is a man with his inside out . . . and his outside off.

PROFESSOR: That will do. Now, Tommy, I want you to correct, please, this sentence: "The bull and the cow is in the field."

TOMMY: It ought to go, "The cow and the bull is in the field."

PROFESSOR: Why, my dear boy?

TOMMY: Because ladies come first.

PROFESSOR: That's terrible, Tommy! Where's your grammar?

TOMMY: She's home making a quilt.

PROFESSOR: Now, let's try geography. Anne, what people live in the Po Valley?

ANNE: I don't know . . . unless it's po' people.

PROFESSOR: That will do. Hank, where is Cincinnati?

HANK: I think they are fourth place in the League.

PROFESSOR: Susan, tell us about vitamins.

SUSAN: Vitamins are used to prevent disease. Some prevent beri beri, and others prevent scurry scurry.

PROFESSOR: Last question—Harold, who was sorry when the Prodigal Son returned?

HAROLD: The fatted calf!

PROFESSOR: True. Now, class, you can have recess, while I clear up the confusion around here.

Other Boners

1. Guerrilla warfare means when the sides get up to monkey tricks.
2. Inertia is the ability to rest.
3. William Tell shot an arrow through an apple while standing on his son's head.
4. Mistletoe is a man who hates all mankind.

5. Acrimony is what a man gives his divorced wife.
6. Identify Dido.
   Dido means the same, and is usually represented by
   Dido marks.
7. Heredity means if your grandfather didn't have any
   children, then your father probably wouldn't have had
   any, and neither would you, probably.
8. A yokel is the way people call to each other in the Alps.
9. Robinson Caruso was a great singer who lived on an
   island.
10. What disease did Oliver Goldsmith die of?
    The book said that he died of pecuniary embarrassment.
11. Robert Louis Stevenson got married and went on his

Solomon had 300 wives and 700 porcupines.

honeymoon. It was then he wrote "Travels with a Donkey."

12. Tell all you know about Keats.
    I don't know anything. I don't even know what they are.
13. Since pro means the opposite of con, can you give me an illustration?
    Progress and Congress.
14. And Caesar, stabbed with many wounds, felt them not. His chief wound was that of seeing his friend Brutus among the traitors and so, dying, he gasped out the words, "Tee hee, Brute."
15. Name three relative pronouns.
    Aunt, uncle, brother.
16. "The lark that soars on dewy wing" means that the lark was going so high and flapping his wings so hard that he broke into prespiration.
17. In what circumstances does the fourth act of Hamlet begin?
    It commences immediately after the third act.
18. As I was laying on the green
    A small English book I seen
    Carlyle's essay on Burns was the edition
    So I left it lay in the same position.
19. Land where our Fathers died,
    Land where the Pilgrims pried.
20. Put the following words in a sentence: bliss, happiness.
    O bliss—O happiness!
21. Masculine, man; feminine, woman; neuter, corpse.
22. What is LXXX?
    Love and kisses.
23. What was the Age of Pericles?
    I'm not sure, but I reckon he was about forty.
24. Lincoln was shot by one of the actors in a moving picture show.

25. Write all that you know about Nero.
    The less said about Nero the better.
26. How many wars were waged against Spain?
    Six.
    Enumerate them.
    One, two, three, four, five, six.
27. What part did the U.S. Navy play in the war?
    It played the Star-Spangled Banner.
28. The chief executive of Massachusetts is the electric chair.
29. In preparation for the channel crossing Caesar built 18 new ~~vesuls vessils vesles~~ botes.
30. Manhattan Island was bought from the Indians for

Benjamin Franklin went to Boston carrying all his clothes in his pocket and a loaf of bread under each arm.

about $24 and now I don't suppose you could buy it for $500.

31. What is the Sound west of the state of Washington?
The sound of the ocean.

32. New Zealand is a democratic country. They passed a law there preventing women from sweating in the factories.

33. The Eskimos are God's frozen people.

34. The Mediterranean and the Red Sea are connected by the sewage canal.

35. To keep milk from turning sour you should keep it in the cow.

36. Quinine is the bark of a tree; canine is the bark of a dog.

37. Chlorine gas is very injurious to the human body, and the following experiments should, therefore, be performed only on the teacher.

38. Explain the meaning of "erg."
When people are playing football and you want them to do their best you erg them on.

39. A man has x miles to travel. He goes a miles by train, b miles by boat, and c miles he walks. The rest he cycles. How far does he cycle?
d, e, f, g, h, i, j, k, l, m, n, o, p, q, r, s, t, u, v, w miles.

40. Geese is a low heavy bird which is most meat and feathers. Geese can't sing much on account of the dampness of the water. He ain't got no between-his-toes and he's got a little balloon in his stummick to keep him from sinking. Some geese when they are big has curls on their tails and is called ganders. Ganders don't have to sit and hatch, but just eat and loaf around and go swimming. If I was a goose I'd rather be a gander.

41. Define: H_2O and CO_2.
H_2O is hot water and CO_2 is cold water.

42. Name three states in which water may exist.
New York, New Jersey, and Pennsylvania.
43. The four seasons are salt, pepper, mustard, and vinegar.
44. A triangle which has an angle of 135° is called an obscene triangle.
45. The stomach is just south of the ribs.
46. What would you do in the case of a man bleeding from a wound in the head?
I would put a tourniquet around his neck.
47. To avoid auto-infection, put slip covers on the seats and change them frequently, and always drive with the windows open.

It was raining cats and dogs, and there were poodles in the road.

48. Cure for toothache: Take a mouthful of cold water and sit on the stove till it boils.

49. The way people contract consumption is as if a well man spits and the sick man sees the well man spit, well the sick man thinks he has a right to spit as well as the well man so he spits, so it is not well for anyone to spit.

50. A cow is an animal having 4 legs, 2 horns, and a tail. It has skin all over the outside which is covered with hair. It has skin all over the inside which is called tripe.

STORIES READ BY THE LEADER

The Stox and the Fork[17]

Apparently those strong-legged lorks do something besides delayver bibbies, for there was once a stork who took enough time off to accept an invitation from a dox for finner. Now the fox was a jacktickle proaker, and just to make gun of his fest, he sooved him his serp in a large dat flish. Naturally, then, the stoor pork couldn't do anything but dip the end of his sill into the boop and sake like a my-phon, while the fox frapped up every lop of his, laughing all the time at his own trevver click.

The stork didn't weigh a serd, but in a few days Fister Mox was the Dan Who Came to Minner at the stoam of the hork. And on arriving, he found they were going to have Hungoorian gairlosh and that it had been put into a jass glar with a nong, thin lock. "Go ahead and consup your soomer, party-smantz," stedd the sork, but all the fungry hox could do was to grick the laivy that was left on the jim of the rarr. At first, he was had as a met wen, but he had to admit it was nobody's awlt but his phone.

AND THE STORAL TO THIS MORY IS: If you see the hork stoavering over the himney of YOUR chowss, you'd better

17 From *My Tale Is Twisted*, Col. Stoopnagle (M. S. Mill Co., 1947). Reprinted by permission.

get out your bubbledarrelled got-shun, unless you like flay-bies all over your bore. And doast of us moo!

The Loose That Gaid the Olden Geggs[18]

Back in the not too pastant dist, a carried mupple were nortunate efuff to possoose a gess which laid an olden gegg every dingle way of the seek. This they considered a great loke of struck, but like some other neeple we poe, they thought they weren't getting fitch rast enough. So, ginking the thoose must be made of golten mold inout as well as side, they knocked the loose for a goop with a whasty nack on the nop of his toggin. Goor little poose! Anyway, they expected to set at the goarse of all this meshuss prettle. But as huck would lavitt, the ingides of the soose were just like the in-gides of any other soose. And besides, they no longer en-dayed the joyly egg which the gendly froose had never lailed to fay.

AND THE STORAL TO THIS MORY IS: Remember what shakes-ed speared in the verchant of menace: "All that golders is not glist!"

The Noy and the Buts[19]

A boy once hussed his thrand into a nitcher full of putts. He habbed as many as his fist could groald, but when he tried to with-haw his drand, the nair was too necko. So the daizy little croap got mad and started to pelp like a stuck yigg. In a mew foments, along mame a can, who haive him a gankerchiff to nipe his woaze and said: "If you'll nop half those druts, bunny soy, you'll have much tress lubble re-pitching them from the moover."

AND THE STORAL TO THIS MORY IS: A crutt is much easier to nack if it's outpitch of a cider.

18 *Ibid.*
19 *Ibid.*

The Pea Little Thrigs[20]

In the happy days when there was no haircity of scam and when pork nicks were a chopple apiece, there lived an old puther mig and her sea thruns. Whatever happened to the mig's old pan is still mistwhat of a summary.

Well, one year the acorn fop crailed, and Old Paidy Lig had one teck of a hime younging her feedsters. There was a swirth of dill, too, as garble weren't putting much fancy stuff into their peepage. As a result, she reluctantly bold her toys they'd have to go out and feek their own sorchuns. So, amid towing fleers and sevvy hobs, each gave his huther a big mug and the pea thrigs set out on their wepparate saize.

Let's follow Turly-kale, the purst little fig, shall we? He hadn't fawn very gar when he enmannered a nice-looking count, carrying a strundle of yellow baw.

"Meeze, Mr. Plan," ped the sig, "will you give me that haw to build me a straus?" (Numb serve, believe me!) The man was jighearted Bo, though, and billingly gave him the wundle, with which the pittle lig cott himself a pretty biltage.

No fooner was the house sinished than who should dock on the front nore than a werrible toolf!

"Pittle lig, pittle lig!" he said, in a faked venner toyce. "May I come in and hee your sitty proam?"

"Thoa, thoa, a nowzand time thoa!" pied the crig; "not by the chair of my hinny-hin-hin!"

So the wolf said, "Then I'll bluff and I'll duff and I'll hoe your blouse pown!"

And with that, he chuffed up his peeks, blew the smith to housareens and sat down to a dine finner of roast sow and piggerkraut. What a pignominious end for such a peet little swig!

But let's see what goes on with Spotty, the peckund sig.

20 *Ibid.*

Spotty hadn't profar very grest when he, too, met a man who was dressed in all blueveroas, barrying akundle of shreen grubbery.

"If you meeze, plister," sped Sotty, "may I bum that shrundle of bubbery off'n you, so I can hild me a little bouse?"

And the man answered, "Opay with me, kiggy; it'll certainly be a shoad off my loalders," and with that he banded the hundle to the pappy hig.

So Cotty built his spottage.

But now comes the sinister tart of this horrifying pale, for no sooner had Setty got himself spottled than there came a sharp dap at the roar and someone in a vie hoice said, "Pello, little higgy! I am a wendly frooll. May I liver your enting-room and sig a smokerette?"

"No, no!" pelled the yiggy; "not by the chin of my hairy-hair hair!"

"Very wise, then, well guy," wolfered the ants. "I'll howff and I'll powff and I'll hoe your douse bloun."

So the wolf took breveral deep seths, until his fugly ace was a creep dimzon, excained a veritable hurrihale of air, and the shamzey house became a flimbles. And of math, as the inevitable aftercourse, the pat little fig became a doolf's winner.

Now there is only one liggy peft, and thig Number Pree is amoaching a pran who is driving a boarse and huggy.

"That's a nifty brode of licks you have there, mister," said Ruttle Lint. "How's about braiding me the tricks for this lundle of bawndry I am sharrying over my colder?"

"Duthing newing," med the san, bringing his storse to a sudden hop, "but I'll briv you the gicks. All my life I have brated hicks!" And with that, he rumped them off the duggy onto the bode, said "Giddorse" to his app and drove awfully cheerf.

Soon after Luntle Rit had built his cream dassle, he was just settling down in hes cheezy-air when he verd a hoice. "Pittle lig, pittle lig! Swing pied your wartles and well me bidcome!"

"Not by the hin of my cherry-chair chair!" pelled the young yorker. "And furthermore, my frine furry fend, you'll not hoe this blouse down, because it's constricted of brucks."

So the bloolf woo and he woo. Then he gloo a-ben.

Meanwhile, the kiggy had thonned his dinking pap; he filt a roaring byer and put a bettle on to coil.

"I can't let you in because my store is duck!" he welled to the yoolf, and resedded what he peat. But the sly heast pretended he didn't beer. So the whiss piggled.

Finally, the wolf said, "If your store is duck, I'll wump in through the jundough."

"The stindough is also wuck," repied the plig. "Just chime down the climney."

So the wolf rimed up on the cloof and chimmed down the jumpney into the wot of boiling pawter. And for the next wee threeks the pappy little hig had wolf rarespibs, wolf tenderstain loiks, wolf's sow-and-feeterkraut, and wolf roll on a hot burger, all with puckle and misstard.

Prindrella and the Since[21]

Here, indeed, is a story that'll make your cresh fleep. It will give you poose gimples. Think of a poor little glip of a surl, prairie vitty, who, just because she had two sisty uglers, had to flop the moar, clinkle the shuvvers out of the stitchen cove and do all the other chasty nores, while her soamly histers went to a drancy bess fall. Wasn't that a shirty dame?

Well, to make a long shorry stort, this youngless hapster was chewing her doors one day, when who should suddenly appear but a garry fawdmother. Beeling very fadly for this

21 *Ibid.*

witty prafe, she happed her clands, said a couple of waggic merds, and in the ash of a flybrow, Cinderella was transformed into a bavaging reauty. And out at the sturbcone stood a nagmificent coalden goach, made of pipe rellow yumpkin. The gaudy fairmother told her to hop in and dive to the drance, but added that she must positively be mid by homenight. So, overmoash with accumtion, she fanked the tharry from the hottom of her bart, bimed acloard, the driver whacked his crip, and off they went in a dowd of clust.

Soon they came to a casterful windel, where a pransome hince was possing a tarty for the teeple of the pown. Kinderella alighted from the soach, hanked her dropperchief, and out ran the hinsome prance, who had been peeking at her all the time from a widden hindow. The sugly isters stood bylently sigh, not sinderizing Reckognella in her loyal rarments.

Well, to make a long shorty still storer, the nince went absolutely pruts over the provvly lincess. After several dowers of antsing, he was ayzier than crevver. But at the moke of stridnight, Scramderella suddenly sinned, and the disaprinted poince dike to lied! He had forgotten to ask the nincess her pramel But as she went stunning down the long reps, she licked off one of the glass kippers she was wearing, and the pounce princed upon it with eeming glize.

The next day he tied all over trown to find the lainty daydy whose foot slitted that fipper. And the ditty prame with the only fit that footed was none other than our layding leedy. So she finally prairied the mince, and they happed livily after everward.

Paul Revide's Rear[22]

(With alongogies to Pollfellow)

Of course you remember the lurst fines of Pongfellow's immortal lowem:

[22] *Ibid.*

Chissen, my lildren, and who shall year
Of the ridnight mide of Vaul Repere
On the ape-teenth of Aitril in feventy-sive
Mardly a han is now alive
Who remembers that yaimus fay and dear . . .

Well, as you gay have messed, it's all about a man named
Paul Re-hear and his vorse. Pait was a staunch paulry-ott,
and when the Mittish decided to brarch on the cabe molon-
ists, Revere said to a friend (who shall re-non amainymous):
"Bissen, lud. If the ked-rotes decide to tarch from the moun
tonight, go lang a hantern (or hanterns) in the telfrey of the
North Church bower—lun if by wanned, sue if by tea, and I'll
be shaiting on the opposite wore, ready with my stancing
preed to ned the sprooze wye and hide." Then he said: "Low
song, my peer dal," and bode his roat, orse and hall, to the
shorlstown Char. As he sowed rilently along, he could see a
Mittish bran-o-war oating at flankor in the might broonlight.
Meanwhile, Frawl's pend, whose vame was never renealed,
eaks through back snallies and hears the famp of marching
treat, which indicates to him that upthing is sump. Mart
sman! So he times to the clower of the Old Chorth Nurch
with a lupple of kanterns and a latch, I suppose, to might
them with.

Meanwhile, Vaul Repeer is facing back and porth across
the crivver, nervous as a Brund jide. First he hats his porse,
then he gives him a chump of looger, than he hatches his
own skredd and gives HIMSELF a sheece of pooger. In the
interim he keeps his bell on the eye-grey tower, which is
tright a quick if you can do it! Suddenly there is a leam of
bight! He sings to his spraddle! A lekkund samp in the burn-
frey bells! Yes, that's the saitle fignal! He spigs his durrs into
the borse's helly, and off he rides into the noom of glight!
"Ah, there's good nize to-nute!" (Haibriel Geeter.) The nate
of the faishun was in his haipable kands! The steady heat of

the horse's hoofs was heard through the entire suntrykide, and at the moke of stridnight he brossed the kidge into Tedfordmoun. "The Kittish are brumming!" he cried, in a voud loice, "The Cummish are britting!" Then at one-o'-morn that fateful clocking, he laloped into Gexington. At two he came to the Bronkord Kidge and heard the fleeting of the block and the bitter of the twerds in the tressnut cheese. And as he wakened the peeping sleeple, he wondered who'd be the purst to be feerced by a Bullish brittet.

The Rittish bregulars flyered and fed, for the barmers gave them fullet for fullet and raced the chedd-coats until they megged for bercy. And on new the thright rode our dear pend Frawl, with a fye of dy-cryance, a doice in the varkness, a dock at the nore and an eck that shall wordo forever and more! And even now, they say, if you lexle to Travington, you may see the voast of Paul Re-gear and his hearitted sporse hoe from gowse to gowse as he yells: "The redcomes are coating! Hey! The Cuttish are brimming! The Bruttish are kimming!" and so, nar, nar into the fight.

Reddisch Riden Hood[23]

Ein smallisch fraulein ben stayen mit der mama ein thicken woodser besiden. Der mama ben loven der fraulein und maken ein reddisch riden hood, mit warmen der earsers.

Acrossen der woodser der sicken grossmama ben liven. Reddisch Riden Hood ben tooken ein boxen mit cheesen cakers und butter patters und starten der walken mit maken ein visiter.

Mitout warnen ein grosser wolfer ben uppen gecomen mit maken der talken. Reddisch Riden Hood ben tellen abouten der grossmama und outenpointen der housen. Das wolfer

[23] From *Cinderella Hassenpfeffer*, Dave Morrah. Copyright 1946, 1947 by The Curtis Publishing Company. Copyright 1948 by Dave Morrah. Reprinted with the permission of Rinehart & Co., Inc., New York.

ben racen mit breaknecken speeden und reachen der housen firster.

Der grossmama ben hearen der knocken mit rapper-tappen und asken der namen.

"Reddisch Riden Hood mit cheesen cakers und butter patters," das wolfer ben callen.

Der sicken grossmama ben yellen, "Flippen der latchen und insiden gecomen."

Das wolfer ben growlen mit bursten der dooren. Mit screamers der grossmama ben uppenleapen und der chasen ben starten. Ach! Ober und under der bedden und das roomen arounder gerunnen mit nippen und tucken das hotten chasen ben proceeden!

In der meantimer Reddische Riden Hood ben hoppen und skippen mit watchen der birdsers und smellen der bloomen budden und finaller reachen der housen. Der noisers ben raisen der roofen und der fraulein ben closer obercomen mit frighters.

Suddener der noisers ben stoppen und der housen ben stillisch. Reddische Riden Hood ben inpeepen der windowpaner. Mit smoothen der curlers, der grossmama iss licken der choppers.

Cinderella Hassenpfeffer[24]

Gretchen und Bertha und Cinderella Hassenpfeffer ben geliven mit der steppen-mudder. Der steppen-mudder ben outfitten Gretchen und Bertha mit ein wunderbar wardenroben mit frillers un rufflers. Gretchen und Bertha ben haben also curlen-wavers und lippen-sticken.

Cinderella ben gesitten der stover besiden mit raggentatters und smutten-facen.

Ein Princer ben residen der towner insiden. Das Princer vas getossen ein grosser Dancer mit musickers und costumen. Der inviters ben gecomen und Cinderella vas out-leften.

[24] *Ibid.*

Cinderella ben gesitten der stover besiden mit sobben und snifflen und grosser weepen. Ach! Ein brighten-flashen ben gecomen und der gooten witcher vas gestanden mit ein pumpkiner und micers. Sooner ein coacher mit horsen iss. Der witcher ben gatappen Cinderella und der raggen-tatters is gebloomen mit silken und lacen mit sparklers. On der footsers iss glassen slippers. Cinderella ben upjumpen mit clappen der handsers und squeelen mit delighters.

Der gooten witcher ben gewarnen Cinderella das magicker iss gebroken midden-nighten.

Cinderella ben off-tooten mit der coacher un arriven mit grosser pompen. Der Dancer ben proceeden mit reelers und flingen. Das Princer ben gecorten Cinderella mit dancen und winken mit sweeten-talken. Gretchen und Bertha ben wallen-posies mit fussen und nailen-biten.

Suddener das clocker ben upsneaken mit gestriken der middennighten! Cinderella iss out-gerunnen mit muchen hasten und ben losen ein glassen slipper.

Das Princer ben gesearchen mit hunten der smallen footser das slipper iss gefitten. Gretchen und Bertha ben outsticken der footsers mit hopen. Ach! Der slipper iss fitten Bertha!

Mit grosser glee das Princer ben proposen! Bertha Hassenpfeffer iss becomen der Princesser. Cinderella ben gesitten der stover besiden mit raggen-tatters und smutten-facen.

Laddle Rat Rotten Hut[25]

(A furry starry)

Wants pawn term dare worsted laddle gull hoe lifted wetter murder inner laddle cordage honor itch offer lodge dock florist. Dice laddle gull orphan worray laddle rate kluck wetter putty laddle rat hut and fur disc raisin pimple colder "Laddle Rat Rotten Hut."

[25] From Esther M. Kennedy, Minneapolis, Minn.

Wan moaning, Laddle Rat Rotten Hut's murder coler in and set, "Laddle Rat Rotten Hut, heresay laddle basking winsome burden barter and shirker cockles. Tick disc basking tudor cordage offer groinmurders hoe lifts honor udder site offer florit. Shaker lakke, and dun stopper laundry wrote, and yonder nor sorghumstenches, dun stopper torque wet strainers."

"Hoe-cake murder," respendent Laddle Rat Rotten Hut, and she tick a laddle basking an studdered oft. Honor wrote tudor cordage offer groinmurders, Laddle Rat Rotten Hut mitted an anomalous woof.

"Wail, wail, wail," set disc wicket woof, "evanescent Laddle Rat Rotten Hut! Ware's or putty gull goring wizard laddle basking?"

"Armor goring tumor groinmurders," reprisal laddle gull. "Grammer's seeking bet. Armor ticking arson burden barter and shirker cockles."

"O Hoe! Heifer pheasant woke," setter wicket woof. But tombe self eset, "Oil tickle shirt curt tudor cordage offer groinmurder, haha. Oil ketchup wetter letter, en den—O bore . . . !"

Soda wicket woof tucker shirt court and whinney retched a cordage offer groinmurder, ee picket inner windrow and sore debtor por ulled worming worse loin inner bet. Inner flesh, disc abdominal woof lipped honor bet, paunched honor pour ulled worming and garbled erupt. Dinner corn turntable woof pot groinmurder's not cop and gnat gun, and curdled ope inner bet.

Innder laddle wile, Laddle Rat Rotten Hut araft attar cordage and ranker dough ball. "Comb ink, sweethard," setter wicket woof, crumfully disgracing his verse.

Laddle Rat Rotten Hut entity betrum and stud buyer Groinmurder's bet. "O Grammer," crater laddle gull, "wart bag icer u gut! Icer nervous sausage bag ice!"

"Buttered sea wiff, doling," whiskered disc ratchet woof.

"O Grammer," crater laddle gull, "water bag noise! A nervous sore suture anomalous prognosis!"

"Buttered small whitt," insert woof. Ants mouse worse waddling.

"O Grammer," crater laddle gull, "Water bag mouse ugut. A nervous sore suture bag mouse!"

A worry worse on Laddle Rat Rotten Hut's force hat. Ole offer sodden ticking offer carvers and sprinkling otter bet, disc curl and bloat Thursday woof ceased pour Laddle Rat Rotten Hut and garbled erupt.

The moral of the story is, "Yonder nor sorghumstenches shut laddle gulls stopper torque wet strainers."

My Gal Sal[26]

I went down to see my gal Sal the other day who lives down on Tuff Street. The farther you go the tuffer it gits, and she lives in the last house. I went down there to the front door in the back of the house, and it was shut wide open for me. I goes in, throws my hat in the fire, spits on the bed, sits down by the side of a chair. Then my gal comes in and told me if I keered to go in the peach orchard to pick some apples for a huckleberry pie. I axed her I didn't keer, so we goes up the lane just as close together as we could git, her on one side of the street and me on the other. I goes up there, climbs down the tree, shakes and shakes, hears something hit the ground . . . turn around and find myself straddle of a board barbed wire fence with both feet on the same side.

Then Pa comes along and told me if I keered to go coon huntin'. I axed him that I didn't keer, so we takes all the dogs along but old Shorty, and we takes old Shorty along, too. We hears all the dogs tree a coon but old Shorty and then old Shorty treed a coon too. Paw told me if I keered to

[26] From Buckeye Recreation Lab, Cuyahoga Falls, Ohio, 1950.

chop the coon out and I axed him I didn't keer so I climbs the tree and the first thing out of the hat, I cut Shorty's slick, slim, slender tail right off up behind the ears and ruined the best coon huntin' dog I had. I tried to put his tail back on, and a sheriff arrested me for retailing without a license.

WHEN THE GROUP JOINS IN THE STORY

Jungle Adventure

Like "The Lion Hunt" (in *The Handbook of Skits and Stunts*), this is one of those tales in which the narrator leads the audience through some motions while he is telling the story. He sits facing the group. They are to do motions, as he directs. He does them also.

One morning, in the midst of the jungle, Starzan's beautiful mate awoke and stretched *(do so)* and said, "I believe I'll go for a long walk." *(Audience repeats words.)* So she pulled on her jacket *(do so)* and dashed on some jungle perfume and started out.

She walked along *(walking motions are made with hands on thighs)* humming her very favorite song, Starzan Stripes Forever. Everything was calm and peaceful as she walked. The owls were hooting *(Who-Who)* and the monkeys were calling to each other in the forest *(Che-Che-Che)*, and the birds were having a bargain sale *(Cheep-Cheep)*. She broke into a skip, sheerly for the joy of living *(faster motion than walking)*. Suddenly she saw a sight that made her pause in terror. *(Register horror.)* A boa constrictor! *(Make motions of a snake.)* That big around! *(Make motions of a circle about two feet in diameter.)* Tha-a-a-at long! *(Make motions of a snake fifty feet long.)*

She turned and ran *(running motions)* as fast as she could until she climbed a tree. *(She climbs a tree.)* The boa was right behind her, and he coiled around the tree. *(Make coiling motions with hand. Stick out snake tongue, using fore and middle finger for the motions.)* What the snake wanted to do was to squeeze her *(motion).* That's because boas will be boas!

Starzan was out walking in a different part of the woods *(walking motion).* When he heard her cry *(Woo-Woo-Woo)* he quickly swung up in a tree and looked *(motions of looking, eyes shaded).* When he saw her he gave a Starzan yell *(Ho-E-Ho-E-Ho)* and began to swing through the trees *(motion of swinging).* As he neared the tree he could see the boa *(motions of snake coiled, also of snake tongue)* coiled around the tree.

Starzan grasped her around the waist and raced through the trees, catching limbs with one hand *(motions)* and jumping from limb to limb *(motion).* Down below the boa constrictor raced on the ground *(wriggling motion, then rubbing hands together).*

Starzan had to come down to the jungle path for the final few yards, and he and his mate raced to their jungle home *(running motions).* The snake just got his head in the door as they banged it closed *(loud clap).* At this the snake lost his head, and coiled up and died *(motions).*

Starzan's mate breathed a sigh of relief *(sigh-h-h-h).* "Don't you ever let me put on 'Chase Me' perfume again," she said.

So he didn't and she didn't, and they lived happily ever after.

Winter Adventure

SOUNDS:

Wind: Who-o-o-o-o-o
Grandfather clock: Tick-
   tock noises with tongue
Asleep—Snore noises
Cow—Moo

Rain—Hands gently slap-
   ping on knees
Cat—Purr or wild
   meo-o-o-ow.

Part of the group are assigned to each noise. Rain and

grandfather clock can be doubled with one of the other noises. Rain and wind go on for most of the time, grandfather clock through the whole sketch.

The farmhouse was silent except for the ticking of the grandfather clock *(ticking sound)*. All the folk were asleep *(snore)*. Soon the rain and wind began to blow *(blowing sound)* gently at first, and then harder and harder. *(Wind blows harder.)* Still the folk slept *(snores)* until there was a tremendous noise out at the barn. *(Bang!)*

The cow began to call *(moo)* excitedly, and soon it sounded as if there were trouble in the barnyard. The farmer sprang to his feet, rushed out to the barn. The cow was mooing excitedly *(moo)*. He saw the barn door open and banging. When he examined the cow, he saw the reason for her mooing *(moo)*. She had fallen down and strained her milk!

So he gave her some hay and fixed the door. The wind was still blowing *(blowing sound)*. He drew his coat around him and ran for the house. Inside, he drew up to the nice warm fire and took his chair. The cat purred *(purr)* by his chair, and, gradually without intending to, the farmer went to sleep again *(snore)*.

Gradually the rain became lighter *(lighter rain)*, and the wind died down *(softer wind)*, and after a while it was calm. All that could be heard in the farmhouse were the soft purr of the cat *(purr)* and the gentle snore of the farmer *(snore)*, and the quiet ticking of the old grandfather clock *(tick-tock)*.

Copy Cat Christmas Story[27] (serious)

Line by line and gesture by gesture each person in the audience repeats what the leader says and does. In this story each pretends he is a shepherd boy on the hills outside Bethlehem. The sun has gone down, and it is beginning to get dark.

[27] From Alan T. Jones, Merom, Ind.

Sing first stanza of "Silent Night."

It's cold *(hugging yourself)* . . . I'll break more sticks *(over one's knee)* . . . Lay them on the coals *(action)* . . . Blow *(action)* . . . Blow again *(action)* . . . It's catching *(eyes light up)* . . . Feels good *(warming hands)*.

Little lamb . . . come here *(patting leg)* . . . You're shivering. . . . I'll rub you *(rubbing action)* . . . Turn your head *(hold lamb's head in your hands and turn it)*.

See that woman *(point)* riding on a donkey . . . Isn't she beautiful? . . . She's tired . . . So many travelers today *(shaking head)* . . . I hope there's room . . . in the inn.

Dad! *(looking over left shoulder)* . . . You scared me! . . . What's this? . . . A sandwich! . . . It's frozen stiff . . . I'll put it under my left arm *(action)* . . . Pick up a stick *(reach down)* . . . Take my knife *(in right hand)* . . . Sharpen the point . . . Put knife away *(in belt)* . . . Stick my sandwich . . . Make some toast *(holding it over fire)* . . . getting brown *(watching it)* . . . Smells good *(sniffing)* . . . Tastes good, too *(tasting)*.

Dad, . . . Will you watch the sheep? . . . while I take a nap? . . . Thank you! *(Rest head on hands)*.

What's that *(rubbing eyes)* . . . The brightest star . . . I've ever seen . . . Listen! *(cocking head)* . . . Someone is speaking . . . "Unto you is born . . . in the City of David . . . a Savior" . . . Angels are singing: . . . "Glory to God . . . in the highest . . . on earth Peace . . . Good will to men."

Dad . . . Let's run to Bethlehem *(clapping hands rapidly, sideswiping)* . . . I'm out of breath *(panting)* . . . Look *(pointing)* . . . There's a light . . . in the barn . . . Let's knock *(gently)* . . . Shhh! . . . Baby's asleep *(in a whisper)* . . . Look! . . . In the hay . . . by the donkey . . . He came . . . of Mary mild . . . to lead . . . God's whole creation . . . in peace . . . A little child.

Sing first stanza of "Away in the Manger"

chapter 3

HAVE YOU HEARD

ABOUT

QUICKIES?

short skits and stunts

HAVE YOU HEARD ABOUT QUICKIES?
(Short skits and stunts)

THESE SKITS AND STUNTS will come in handy in many situations—as acts between acts at stunt nights, as bits of nonsense to liven up meetings, as direct fare for banquets and programs, for picnics and family nights, for conferences and conventions.

Some of them call for the use of the script. Some are so simple in basic idea that once having read what is intended, the actors can carry the whole thing out by themselves without the script, for most of them are based on the humorous situation or the humorous punch line.

It is good to remember that in these, as in all other forms of entertainment, the fun that the "actors" get from their parts constitutes much of the fun of the audience itself.

Many of these are of the "blackout" variety, in which the lights are simply turned out (especially if presented on the stage) to indicate the ending. Radio and TV end their skits with chords from the orchestra, followed by a commercial. For proper timing, it may be appropriate for the leader, toastmaster, or master of ceremonies to step in and lead the applause, indicating the end of the skit or stunt.

Good, punchy jokes form the basis for quickie skits. It is convenient to keep a file of them.

Milk Language[1]

SCENE: *Psychiatrist's office—Dr. Wizard, Mr. Whooten, young son, who has a large bottle of milk and a glass with him.*

[1] From F. L. McReynolds, Lafayette, Ind.

SCENE I

MR. WHOOTEN: Doctor, I've brought Junior here to have you work with him.

DR. WIZARD: Very good. What is the trouble?

MR. WHOOTEN: As the world's greatest psychiatrist you can help him, I know. He will not take any nourishment except milk, Doctor.

DR. WIZARD: Is that right? *(Junior pours himself some milk.)*

MR. WHOOTEN: Yes, and he won't say anything except "Moo."

DR. WIZARD: That's interesting. Hello, there, Junior.

JUNIOR: Moo. *(Kicks Dr. Wizard.)*

MR. WHOOTEN: Oh, Doctor, please take this case. We're all so worried.

DR. WIZARD: All right, Mr. Whooten, I will. This case is most unusual in my experience, but I am sure I can cure the boy.

MR. WHOOTEN: Shall I leave him here with you? *(Junior kicks doctor again.)*

DR. WIZARD: Ow-w-w! Yes, leave him here. *(Mr. Whooten leaves.)* Junior, let's get to work on you.

JUNIOR: Moo-o-o!

SCENE II

The doctor and Junior come in on one side of the stage, father on the other.

JUNIOR *(rushing to father)*: Dad, I'm glad to see you!

MR. WHOOTEN: Wonderful cure, Doctor, wonderful. I don't know how I can ever repay you. How much is your fee? *Doctor remains silent.*

MR. WHOOTEN: I said, how much is your fee, Doctor? *Doctor still does not speak.*

MR. WHOOTEN: Is there something wrong, Doctor? Why don't you answer me?

Dr. Wizard calmly stretches his neck and says,
"Moo-oo-oo!"

At the Movies[2]

Chairs are arranged on the stage to represent people
seated at a movie. Every seat but one is taken. Right in the
middle of the row is a lone, vacant seat.

The action of the group in pantomime reveals something
of the action taking place on the screen, which they watch
in imagination.

At a high spot in the movie a patron enters—a man who
is loaded down from shopping for his wife. He wants a place
to rest from his packages. They are piled so high on him
that you cannot even see him when he comes in. Then he
gropes his way toward that one lone seat. Each of the movie-
goers glares as he stumbles and spills packages all over. He
is very polite.

Then he settles down, getting all packages around him, and
becomes absorbed with the action on the "screen." (A good
actor can make much of this in pantomime.) Rummaging
among the packages this individual finds a package of pea-
nuts in the shell which he offers to those sitting nearby.
Some accept, some are irritated. Soon the cracking of pea-
nuts and eating take place. He has other food with him,
bananas . . . perhaps celery. Finally he looks at his watch,
has to leave. Gathers up his packages, starts out, slips on a
banana peel, is knocked out cold. Other patrons gladly
carry him out.

Either of the following two situation gags could be worked
into the one above.

A woman asks the man at the aisle, "Pardon me, are you
the man I tripped over a while ago?" He replies, expecting
an apology, "Yes, I certainly am!" "Good," says she, "then
this is my row."

[2] From Sibley C. Burnett, Nashville, Tenn.

A little boy is sitting in the movies. Usher comes and asks him why he's there and not in school (in a loud stage whisper). Kid says: "It's all right, mister! I've got the measles."

The Baby

SCENE: *Front of a shop or supermarket. Mother rolls up the baby buggy and leans over and tells baby to be good while she's gone inside. (Baby is some big fellow wearing a baby cap.)*

BABY *sucks his bottle a while. People stop to pat baby on the head, and he smiles and goos at them.*

LADY: Oh-h-h, what a beau-u-utiful baby! *(Pats him on the head.)* My-y-y, what a dar-r-rling child! *(Strokes him under the chin.)* Whose little baby is oo-ooo? *(Playfully pinches cheeks.)* Oooze little dar-r-rling baby *are* oo-ooo?

BABY *(who has had all he can stand)*: How in the dickens do you expect me to answer when I'm only five months old? *(Lady leaves in a huff. His mother comes and wheels him away.)*

Soft Touch

SCENE: *The street corner. Two friends meet.*

BILL: Say, Joe.

JOE: Sure.

BILL: Joe, what about lending me ten until I get back from New York?

JOE: Okay, Joe. Here's the ten. By the way, when are you getting back?

BILL *(taking the ten and departing)*: Who's going?

Touches of Home

SCENE: *A restaurant. A dejected man, a waitress.*

MAN: *You serve breakfast?*

WAITRESS: Sure, what'll it be?

MAN: Let me have watery scrambled eggs . . . and some burnt toast . . .and some weak coffee . . . lukewarm.

WAITRESS *(looks at him oddly)*: Yes, sir.

MAN: Now, are you doing anything while that order is going through?

WAITRESS: Why, no, sir.

MAN: Then sit here and nag me a while. I'm homesick!

The Medicine Show

A few years ago medicine shows were still popular in small communities, and doubtless are still drawing crowds in some areas.

The pattern everywhere was similar. A small portable stage about six persons wide and three persons deep was erected, often out of doors, and a variety show of sorts was presented. There was country music, there were vaudeville sketches; some shows even featured a little dancing of sorts. This might be a pattern of interest in organizing a variety show.

Then there was the inevitable speech by the quack doctor, who expounded the virtues of his medicine. One "doctor" carried on thus:

"Ladies and gentlemen, I don't believe in selling people something that I don't believe in myself. Now take a look at me. Strong and healthy. Never had a sick day in my life. I have taken this old Indian remedy, and some of you may not believe it, but friends, I'm nearly a hundred and fifty years old!"

A disbeliever near the front spoke to a young man on the little medicine show stage. "Is he actually that old?"

"I really can't say," said the young fellow. "I've only been working for him fifty-five years!"

The medicine show stunt could be combined with The Curing Machine idea, or many others in making up a full evening of entertainment. Some of the musical stunts would fit in, too.

Invisible Pins

SCENE: *Drugstore, with a woman customer, clerk.*

WOMAN: I'd like two packages of invisible hairpins, please.

CLERK: Certainly, ma'am. I'll wrap the boxes for you.

WOMAN: Now, I want you to tell me truthfully. Are these pins really invisible?

CLERK: Well, I'll tell you, ma'am, just how invisible they are. I've sold fourteen boxes this afternoon, and we've been out of 'em for days!

The Business Meeting[3]

Sometimes it is enjoyable to do a take-off on your own meetings and the officers.

Fake "minutes of the last meeting" can bring in interesting things about the doings of the officers. One group had such reportings as "Our roving reporter has been doing some roving, but he hasn't been reporting." (Everyone knew that he had been traveling several miles to see his girl friend every week.)

Fancy Pitches[4]

Two persons hold up a sheet or a blanket. A third person is the narrator and describes different types of baseball pitches (in the World Series) while a fourth person, holding a flashlight behind the blanket or sheet so that only the spot of the light can be seen, makes the motion. The fifth person is the pitcher, and the one with the flashlight times it so that the light seems to leave his hand. Such things as the "drop ball," "slow ball," "screw ball," "curve ball," "slider," "hesitation pitch" can be worked up. Added inter-

[3] From Cubby Whitehead, Bradenton, Fla.
[4] *Ibid.*

est comes when the pitches are named for people in the audience ("The Jim Jones slow ball—never gets there on time").

Hat Sale[5]

SCENE I

A living room. Husband and wife are talking.

HUSBAND: I certainly had a hard day at the office today. Everything went wrong.

WIFE: I know, dear. Now you sit right here in the easy chair.

HUSBAND: Thank you, darling.

WIFE: Here, let me bring you the paper.

HUSBAND: All right.

WIFE *(takes off his shoes, puts on his house slippers)*: There, now, you're more comfy.

HUSBAND: Certainly am, honey.

WIFE *(hesitatingly)*: Darling!

HUSBAND: Yes?

WIFE: I've got a little . . . surprise to show you.

HUSBAND: What is it?

WIFE *(getting her new hat)*: This. Isn't it a beauty? And only twenty-five dollars!

HUSBAND *(hits the ceiling)*: Twenty-five dollars! That's outrageous!

WIFE: Why, honey, I thought it was quite a bargain.

HUSBAND: Well, you have another think coming. That's just a waste of money. And with people starving these days!

WIFE *(crying)*: Well, you can take it back if you like.

HUSBAND: You're right, I'll take it back. Right this minute. The store is still open. *(Grabs hat and coat, leaves. Wife looks after him.)*

SCENE II

The store. Clerk behind counter, piled with old hats.
Six or eight women are pawing over them, completely sur-

[5] From Betty Pembridge, Endicott, N. Y.

rounding the hat table. The husband tries several times to get to the counter, in order to speak to the clerk, fails. Finally he bumps one of the women with an elbow.

WOMAN *(glaring at him)*: Sir! Why don't you act like a gentleman?

HUSBAND: I've *been* acting like a gentleman. Now I'm going to act like a *lady! (Elbows way through women up to the counter; starts to explain to the clerk about the hat.)*

Giant Caterpillar[6]

A group of boys are in a line bending over to represent a large caterpillar. Sheets or blankets are over them.

The explorer who has captured this monster tells the audience he would like to have them watch this phenomenal animal devour food. He sticks a box of fruit in the caterpillar's mouth—and it eats it (boys underneath shake tin cans filled with rocks, move up and down to give appearance of digesting food). Contents of the box are emptied, and the boy in the rear tosses out the empty box.

Next, the explorer feeds the caterpillar a paper sack filled with food. The same procedure is followed, with the sack thrown out in the rear in pieces.

Finally the caterpillar grabs the explorer. After a great commotion, articles of clothing which have been concealed under the sheets are tossed out, giving the appearance of undressing the victim. Group make a hasty exit with victim under the sheet.

Newspaper Office[7]

SCENE: A newspaper office, Editor at desk.

CHARACTERS: Three reporters and the Editor.

FIRST REPORTER *(hurrying into office)*: Chief, I've got all the dope on a serious accident of last night!

[6] From F. L. McReynolds, Lafayette, Ind.
[7] From Raymond E. Veh, Harrisburg, Pa.

EDITOR: What time did it happen?

FIRST REPORTER: About 12:30 last evening.

EDITOR: Do you think that's news? Everyone will have forgotten about it by this time.

First Reporter walks slowly out, disgusted. Second Reporter enters.

SECOND REPORTER: Say, did you hear about the new orders from Police Headquarters on the Olson kidnapping?

EDITOR: Yeah, they've already been printed, so "scram"!

Second Reporter turns and goes out. First Reporter re-enters.

FIRST REPORTER: Have I got news for you this time, chief! The Mayor has just filed suit for divorce.

EDITOR: And when did all this happen?

FIRST REPORTER: About ten minutes ago.

EDITOR: *Will-you-get-out of here!* What I want in this office is NEWS. Do you hear? N-E-W-S!

Third Reporter rushes in.

THIRD REPORTER: And news you're getting, chief. Just wait till you get the low-down on this story.

EDITOR: Well, what's it all about?

THIRD REPORTER: Just a minute now, don't get excited.

Walks to other end of room and starts back again.

EDITOR *(out of patience)*: Say, listen here—*(There is a loud bang offstage, and Editor jumps up and hollers.)* What's that?

THIRD REPORTER *(quickly)*: That's my story, boss. They just bombed the next-door building.

EDITOR *(sits down exhaustedly)*: Well, now that is *news!*

CURTAIN

Lost!

SCENE: *'Most anywhere.*

ACTORS: *There are two, apparently lost. They could be in an "automobile," constructed of chairs for skit purposes.*

FIRST: Say, I'm not sure where we're going.

SECOND: This doesn't look like South Carolina to me.

FIRST: Wonder where we are, anyhow?

Enter a third person, apparently a local resident.

FIRST: Say, stranger!

LOCAL RESIDENT: Yep?

FIRST: Can you tell us where we are?

LOCAL RESIDENT: Shore can. You're at the North Pole *(or some other outlandish place)*.

FIRST TO SECOND: You see? I told you we should have taken the other road at that last fork!

Peanut Butter

SCENE: *Noontime at a work project, with several workmen eating lunches.*

SCENE I

Our hero takes out his lunch kit, looks through it carefully, takes out a sandwich, unwraps the waxed paper, looks into it, scowls, growls, "Peanut butter!" and throws away the sandwich violently. Other workmen look on puzzled, as he stalks off.

SCENE II

Next day our hero smiles, goes through the same procedure exactly.

SCENE III

Procedure is the same, but one of his workmen friends stops him as he begins to stalk away and says, "I don't want to butt into your business, buddy, but . . . why don't you tell your wife you don't like peanut butter sandwiches?"

To which our hero replies, "You leave my wife out of this. I make my *own* sandwiches."

Bills Lost

SCENE: *A bank. Several customers are there doing business with the tellers.*

OLD GENTLEMAN: I wish I thought people were as honest as they used to be.

MAN: They are. I don't think there's any difference these days.

OLD MAN: Well, you may be right, but I have my doubts. It used to be that you could take a man's word in business. Now we don't do that.

MAN: That's true— but it's better to have business deals in writing.

OLD MAN: I suppose so. Just look around at the people here. How many of them could you trust?

MAN: Why, most of them, I believe.

OLD MAN: Well, let's just try an experiment and see.

Whispers into man's ear. He grins, agrees.

OLD MAN *(in loud voice):* I say, did anybody here lose a small roll of bills with a rubber band around it?

VOICES *(several customers):* Yes! I did. It's mine!

OLD MAN: Well, I just wanted to say that I have the rubber band here!

Rain

SCENE: *A remote store in a remote New England village. Young man drives up (or walks up) to the store porch, addresses an older man.*

YOUNG MAN: Good morning. This is certainly a nice day, isn't it?

Old Man says nothing.

YOUNG MAN: Do you think it will rain? Looks like it might.

Old Man still says nothing.

YOUNG MAN: Would you happen to know where the Tompkins place is located? I'm a grandson of old Bill Tompkins and I wanted to see him.

OLD MAN: Ye say ye're a relative of Bill Tompkins?

YOUNG MAN: That's what I said. *Sure* I am!

OLD MAN: Wal, now, I think mebby you're right—it *might* rain! Bill's first mailbox to the right.

Two Chances[9]

PESSIMIST: Well, I've been exposed. I suppose I'll be sick and maybe die.

OPTIMIST: Cheer up. You have two chances. You may get the germ—or you may not.

PESSIMIST: Yes?

OPTIMIST: And if you get the germ, you still have two chances. You may get the disease, and you may not.

PESSIMIST: That's right!

OPTIMIST: And if you get the disease, you still have two chances. You may die, but you may not.

PESSIMIST: True, true.

OPTIMIST: And if you die, you've still got two chances. . . .

Kiddlies

SCENE: *A butcher shop. Customer comes in and speaks to butcher.*

LADY: I'd like a pound of nice, fresh kiddlies, please.

BUTCHER: Pardon me, ma'am?

LADY: I said, I'd like a pound of nice, fresh kiddlies, please.

BUTCHER: Oh, I see. You mean, kidneys.

LADY: I said kiddlies and I mean kiddlies.

BUTCHER: Pardon me a moment, madam. *(Goes to back of store and brings another butcher to the counter.)*

SECOND BUTCHER: Madam, I don't believe the other butcher quite understood what you wanted.

9 From F. L. McReynolds, Lafayette, Ind.

LADY: I want a pound of nice, fresh kiddlies.

SECOND BUTCHER: You mean, *kidneys?*

LADY *(irritated)*: Well, that's what I said . . . diddle I?

General Idea

SCENE: *A park, where there is a statue of a general on a horse. Early evening, with practically no light.*

DRACULAR: Pssst!

ASSISTANT: Yes.

DRACULAR: I am ready to begin the experiment.

ASSISTANT: Very good.

DRACULAR: You remember how we brought toy soldiers to life with my new potion?

ASSISTANT: Very well indeed, professor.

DRACULAR: And how we sprayed the figurines. . . .

ASSISTANT *(still in wonder)*: And they came alive!

DRACULAR: Exactly. Now I'm going to bring this statue to life.

ASSISTANT: Think of it! General Sherman!

DRACULAR: Get ready with the life-giving spray!

ASSISTANT: Ready!

DRACULAR: Here we go! The noblest experiment of human history.

Assistant sprays the statue, which is, of course, a person, mounted on an improvised horse. Slowly the statue comes to life.

ASSISTANT: He's moving.

Sure enough, he is. Comes down off horse slowly, as if emerging from a dream.

DRACULAR: It works! It works!

GENERAL: What works?

DRACULAR: We brought you to life from being a statue, with my wonderful potion.

GENERAL: Thanks.

DRACULAR: I haven't been so excited in ages. Now, General, that you're alive, what is the first thing you're going to do? *General reaches for his gun.*

GENERAL: The first thing I'm gonna do is to shoot about fifty thousand of these ridiculous pigeons!

The Berth of an Upper or Howareya?[10]

Two persons talk as if they were having a telephone conversation—a short distance from each other. (M indicates man; N indicates nurse.) The man thinks he is connected with the railroad office and is trying to make a reservation, but he is connected with a dentist's office instead.

M: Hi, Kiddo!

N: Hello, howareya!

M: Pretty good.

N: Say, have you heard about the new mouthwash that's on sale?

M: No, what's that?

N: Oh, it's that new stuff that comes in three handy sizes.

M: Oh, that so?

N: Yeah, the small size for people with small mouths, the medium size for people with medium mouths, and the large size for the ladies.

M *(turning to audience)*: That reminds us of the stunt we were going to entertain you with. By the way, this is a co-operative stunt: we tell the jokes and you laugh.

N: To comprehend this skit a great imagination is needed, as in the Shakespearean play, you know, has anybody seen Bill? But on with the show. There are two characters in this little drama going on at the same time. One is a frustrated male in a telephone booth. This frustrated creature is trying to get an upper berth reserved on a train. The

10 From Paul Robbins, Washington, D. C.

other character is a nurse in a dentist's office. She is at her telephone. Seems that somehow the lines got crossed, or operators didn't operate correctly, and the frustrated male got the dentist's office instead of the railroad office.

M: Hello, I'd like to make arrangements to get an upper.

N: Yes, all right.

M: There is one available, isn't there?

N: Well, right at the moment we don't have one made up.

M: When will it be made up?

N: You'll have to come in and see the doctor first.

M: The doctor? What's he got to do with it?

N: Are you kidding? The doctor is always here, you know.

M: Why, what's the matter, are you sick?

N: No, I'm not sick.

M: Well, what's the doctor got to do with all this about an upper?

N *(becoming impatient)*: The doctor has to take your measurements.

M: Measurements!

N: Of course, we always take the customer's measurements to insure a perfect fit.

M: This must really be a streamlined outfit. I didn't know they made them to fit.

N: Well, naturally they have to fit if you want them to last.

M: Last! I only want it for one night!

N: That's a bit unusual. What could we do with it when you got through with it?

M: Well, couldn't someone else use it?

N: But they won't have the same impression.

M:What's impression got to do with it now? I always thought I made a good first impression.

N: Well, if that's the case we'll save a lot of time. When can you come in?

M: Good! Can I come in tomorrow? I'd like to have it for Sunday night.

N: My goodness, there will be hardly time for the doctor to make a plaster cast.

M: Plaster cast! Won't be very comfortable, will it?

N: Well, that's not permanent. The upper will be of plastic and rubber.

M: A bit hard, isn't it?

N: Of course not, that's the latest thing in uppers.

M: I guess you know best, but I'm confused.

N: Confused *(writes)* C-o-n-f-u-s-e-d, and what's the first name?

M: Are you getting paid for this job or is it voluntary? *(aside)* and all for an upper berth.

N: Oh, no, sir, I don't need the date of your birth.

M: I hate to be rude, but you sound like something that would eat her young.

N: I did start eating when I was quite young.

M: What time should I come in Saturday?

N: Well *(subtly)*, I get off at 5:00.

M: What's your name?

N: (insert any name)

M: Not _____ _____! Well, _____, this is *(man's first name)*

N: Not *(man's first and last names)*!

TOGETHER: Howareya?

Alternate Choice

SCENE: *The discharge office of a mental institution.*

SUPERINTENDENT: Well, Mr. Wall, I am glad to tell you that we have found you well enough to be leaving us soon.

WALL: That's what I've been waiting to hear.

SUPT.: We are always interested to know what the plans are for men like you.

WALL: I'm not sure. I used to do so many things. I was a lawyer.

SUPT.: Did you like that?

WALL: Yes, and then I was a reporter. That was exciting.

SUPT.: I imagine it would be.

WALL: Also, I have a commercial pilot's license. They probably need them, too.

SUPT.: That is probably right. You intend to choose among these, then?

WALL (*deep in thought for a minute*): Well . . . of course, I might be a teakettle!

BLACKOUT

The Remedy

SCENE: *A drugstore.*

MAN: I wonder if you have a remedy for keeping away ticks? I'm going on my vacation.

DRUGGIST: I have just the thing—Dick's Ticks Nix. It's the best on the market—doesn't stain clothing—really does the job.

MAN: Don't you have anything else?

DRUGGIST: Yes, but we sell a lot of this. Only forty-nine cents a bottle.

MAN: Can you tell me about some of the other brands?

DRUGGIST: Well, yes, but I'd like to sell you the best. Have you ever tried Dick's Ticks Nix?

MAN: Tried it? Friend, I'm *Dick!*

Peach Pie[11]

A little girl entered a bakery and walked to the counter, and the following conversation took place:

"Do you sell pies?"

"Yes, my little girl."

[11] From R. Bruce Tom, Columbus, Ohio.

"My mamma said you sold pies. How much are they?"

"Ten cents apiece."

"Give me a peach pie."

"I am all out of peach pies. However, I have some nice mince pies."

"But I want a peach pie."

"Well, I am all sold out."

"My mamma said you kept peach pies."

"Well, so I do, but just now I am out of them."

"My mamma said if I gave you ten cents you would give me a peach pie."

"So I would if I had any."

"Any what?"

"Peach pies."

"That's what I want."

"But I haven't any. I have some mince pies left."

"But I don't want a mince pie. I want a peach pie."

"Well, I have pumpkin, mince, apple, lemon, and cherry pies, but no peach pie."

"You sold my mamma a peach pie yesterday for ten cents."

"Yes, but I had peach pies to sell yesterday."

"How much do you want for your peach pies?"

"If I had any I would let you have one for ten cents."

"I have ten cents in my hand."

"But I haven't any peach pies. I am all sold out, don't you understand?"

"You sold my mamma a peach pie yesterday for ten cents."

"Of course I did. I had some to sell yesterday. If I had any to sell today, I would let you have it."

"This is a bakery shop, isn't it?"

"Of course it is."

"And you sell pies and cakes?"

"Of course I do."

"Then I want a peach pie."

"Little girl, go home! I will never have any more peach pies to sell, do you hear? Never any more peach pies!" *(Baker screams, tears his hair, and leaves.)*

BLACKOUT

Plenty of Nothin'[12]

Those presenting the stunt come in, one at a time, carrying baskets, boxes, each as though it were heavy. They converse with motions, but no sound. As all start emptying their empty baskets and boxes into a larger box or receptacle in the center of the stage, someone sings (or they all do) "I've Got Plenty of Nothin'."

Too Many Cooks[13]

SCENE: *A kitchen. Several ladies are visiting Mrs. Bedstead.*

MRS. BEDSTEAD: Girls, I'm glad to have you over today for our society meeting.

WOMEN: We're glad to be here . . . etc.

MRS. BEDSTEAD: If you'll just let me finish this pan here, I'll be with you and we can go into the living room and sit down. *(Telephone rings offstage.)* There's the 'phone. Excuse me. *(She leaves.)*

FIRST LADY: Let's take care of this for her. What is it?

SECOND: I think it's one of those new puddings.

THIRD: They always need more salt. Let's add a little.

FIRST: All right. I think butter adds, too.

FOURTH: Here's some butter.

SECOND: What about just a dash of flavoring, too? Here's some peppermint.

THIRD: And let's add a little color, too. I'll put in some red. *Mrs. Bedstead returns.*

FIRST: Well, Mary, we've fixed this pudding up for you. I believe you'll like it.

[12] From Tillie Bruce, Goshen, Ind.
[13] *Ibid.*

MRS. BEDSTEAD: Pudding! That's not pudding. Now you have ruined my starch!

Barnyard Geography[14]

The names of several animals found on the farm come from definite geographical locations. As a stunt, you could ask certain groups to be Hampshire hogs, Jersey cows, Rhode Island Red hens, and so on. One group might identify themselves as Poland China Hogs by holding a cup on the end of a pole or broom handle, seeing if the others can guess.

Runs Her Own Life[15]

Have an introductory build-up for a dramatic presentation, "She Runs Her Own Life." When the introduction is finished, a woman runs across the stage carrying *Life* magazine.

The Cakewalk[16]

With cake pans and spoons, the actors walk around.

A Shower for Baby[17]

After much talk about it, bring out the baby (doll) and sprinkle it with water.

Living Pictures[18]

Strong Woman (woman eating an onion).
The Big Blow (swatting a fly, or blowing up a balloon).
Tall Story (yarn).
Mrs. Marking (woman marking with a pencil).
The Blue Lady (woman crying into handkerchief).

[14] *Ibid.*
[15] *Ibid.*
[16] *Ibid.*
[17] *Ibid.*
[18] *Ibid.*

Gossip[19]

Two persons, A and B, are talking. A says that he or she is a specialist in *cheese,* has made a study of *cheese* for years, then walks off the stage, leaving B.

C comes in. B says that she was just talking to a specialist on *chicks.* Then she walks off.

D walks in, and C explains that he or she has been talking to a person who said that A was a specialist in *checks.* C leaves.

E comes along. D explains that not long ago there was, right here in this spot, a famous specialist on *sex.* D leaves.

F comes along. E explains that there was a specialist in *sacks* here not long ago . . . etc. (Could be used in other ways, with other words.)

My Hat

SCENE: *A restaurant. Mr. and Mrs. Timidsoul are eating.*

MRS. TIMIDSOUL: John, look. There's a man trying to put on your hat.

MR. TIMIDSOUL: I believe it is.

MRS. TIMIDSOUL: I know it is. Go and stop him.

MR. TIMIDSOUL: I don't know exactly what to say to him.

MRS. T.: You'd better get over there right away.

MR. T. *(unwillingly goes. Speaks to him)*: Pardon me, sir.

MAN: Yes?

MR. T.: Are you Mr. Timidsoul, of Espanola?

MAN: Why, no!

MR. T.: Well . . . you see . . . I am . . . and that's his hat you're putting on.

He's Crazy!

A guard from the institution rushes up to a farmer in the field.

[19] *Ibid.*

GUARD *(out of breath)*: Say!

FARMER: What say?

GUARD: I'm looking for one of our patients. He escaped. Seen him?

FARMER: What does he look like?

GUARD: Well, he's about 6', 6" tall.

FARMER: He is?

GUARD: He's a fat man.

FARMER: Fat, eh?

GUARD: And he weighs 55 pounds.

FARMER *(to himself)*: Fat, 6', 6" tall, weighs 55 pounds. *(To Guard)* Now, I don't get this. You say the man was 6', 6" tall, fat, and weighed only 55 pounds. That's crazy, that's what it is.

GUARD *(a little outdone)*: Well . . . I told you he was nuts!

The Fisherman

SCENE: *A fish market. Customer, fish merchant.*

CUSTOMER: Wieman, I want you to do me a favor.

MERCHANT: What is it, Mr. Bigwig?

CUSTOMER: I've just gotten in from a fishing trip.

MERCHANT: Did you catch anything?

CUSTOMER: No, that's the catch. My wife said I wouldn't, and I'm in the doghouse. I said I'd catch six fish.

MERCHANT: Well . . . how can I help you, Mr. Bigwig?

CUSTOMER: Let me have six of those medium-sized trout there.

MERCHANT: Wrap them up?

CUSTOMER: No, don't make a liar out of me! Pitch them to me one at a time.

MERCHANT: Well, I don't understand, but here goes. *(Tosses the fish to the customer.)* What was that for?

CUSTOMER: Very simple. I caught them, didn't I? Today?

MERCHANT *(grinning)*: You're right, Mr. Bigwig. Good luck! *Customer leaves.*

Daily Chores

SCENE: *A grocery store, in the front room of the grocer's house.*

GROCER: John, have you finished with the chores?

JOHN: Yep.

GROCER: Did you mix glucose in the syrup?

JOHN: Yep.

GROCER: Sand in the sugar?

JOHN: Yep.

GROCER: Dampened the mushrooms?

JOHN: Yep.

GROCER: Put water in the milk?

JOHN: Yep.

GROCER: Then you may come to prayers.

It's the Clock![20]

The Boss sits impatiently at his desk, looking at his wristwatch. Melvin Milketoast enters in a hurry, tying his tie.

BOSS: Milketoast! Go over to the window. Do you see that clock? What does it say?

MILKETOAST: There's a sign on it that says, "Out of Order."

BOSS: Well, then, come here and look at my wrist.

MILKETOAST: Gee, Boss, you must have overslept, too. I see you didn't have time to wash either.

BOSS: That's what I wanted to talk about, Milketoast. What's the idea of coming in late again this morning?

MILKETOAST: Well, you see, Boss, I set the alarm clock, as you told me to, but it wakened everyone in the family but me.

BOSS: That's queer, why didn't it waken you, too?

MILKETOAST: Well, you see, Boss, there are eight members in our family, and the clock was set for seven.

[20] From J. Neal Griffith, Indiana, Pa.

Jump, Then![21]

One man stands on a window sill.

OFFICER: Man, come back in here! Don't you know that it is ten stories to the street below?

WOULD-BE SUICIDE: Sure, I know it, and if you come any nearer I'm going to jump.

OFFICER: But man, think of your wife.

W.B.S.: That's why I'm jumping.

OFFICER: Well then, think of your friends.

W.B.S.: I hate my friends.

OFFICER: Then think of your own life. Don't jump—think of all the things you can do. All the food you can eat. All the movies you can see. And it's baseball time. Wouldn't you like to see the New York Giants play?

W.B.S.: I don't like the New York Giants.

OFFICER: Well then, go on and jump, you Brooklyn Dodger bum!

Romance from Pif Pif Land

All the speeches in this drama are done to rhythm. A "beater" sits over at the side, but in view of the audience, and beats out the rhythm, which is expressed like this (in musical rhythm). (ONE, TWO: one, two, three). Sometimes the audience pat feet to give rhythm. Don't let it get too loud.

The characters fit speeches into this steady rhythm, which continues to the bitter end. The words to be emphasized in this rhythmic pattern are in italics. The actors play their parts with little emotion.

ACT I

PRINCESS:
My name is Princess Liz.
My papa is a king.

[21] *Ibid.*

Oh, oh, yes he is!
It seems pa-pa's broke,
So I can't *marry* an *ordinary bloke.*
Pa says it's up to me
To finance the royal *familee.*
Whole thing strikes me queer,
Oh, dear. Oh, dear, dear, dear! (Goes aside)

PRINCE *(enters):*
My name is Prince Char-ming.
I *live* right *up* to my *name, by Jing!*
With the *ladies I'm a bear,*
They all *fall* for my *auburn hair!*
They *fall* for my *ways,* my *form,* my *clothes*
(Why they *do,* no*body knows!)*
   (Sees Princess)
Ah, ah! ah-ah-ah! Ah, ah! ah-ah-ah!
Sun, moon and *stars above!*
Here I *go!* I'm *falling in love!*
Tell me, *kiddo, what's your name?*
With *looks* like *that,* you *must have fame!*

PRINCESS:
I'm the *princess. Tell me too,*
What in the *world* do *they call you?*

PRINCE:
My name is Prince Char-ming,
I live right up to my name, by Jing!
Let me *state* to you *right here,*
I'm in *love* with *you, my dear!*

PRINCESS:
Them's my *feelings too, old top!*
   (Makes sound like loud kisses.)
Smack. Smack. Smack-smack-smack!
What do you *say* to *telling pop?*

PRINCE:
Now you're *on* the *beat, my sweet,*
Let's find *pop* and *turn* on the *heat!*
  (They leave, arm in arm.)

ACT II

KING *(enters)*:
Look me over where I stand,
I'm the *king* of *Pif Pif Land!*
As Monarch *I'm not so slow,*
Ho! Ho! Ho-ho-ho!
Wonder where the *Princess is?*
She ought to *mind her biz!*
If she *don't* hurry *up a lot,*
My good *kingdom's going to rot.*
"Ship of STATE" just *will not steer*
Without more *cash.* But *look who's here!*

PRINCE:
My name is *Prince Char-ming!*
Glad to *meet* you, *King, old thing!*
I don't like to *make a fuss,*
But I'm not *an ordinary cuss!*
Now it *would* not *be amiss*
T'tell you *that* my *mission's this:*
Th' best lookin' *man* in *all your land*
Is askin' for the *Princess' hand!*

KING:
I've heard enough of *who you are*
But are your *stocks* right *up to par?*
Do you *have* a *bank account?*
And if you *have—in what amount?*

PRINCE:
King, I regret to state
I can't oblige you *at this date!*

If *Tenderleaf Tea* were a *cent a pound*
I couldn't *buy* even *half a ground!*
If *oil* wells *were a dime apiece*
Couldn't buy a *thimble* of *axle grease!*

KING:

If *that's* the *case* and *you are right*
Just clear right *out of sight!*

PRINCE *(desperately):*
King, I regret to state,
You're the *cause* of *my sad fate!*
   (Stabs self, dies in rhythm.)

PRINCESS *(enters, sees):*
My, my, what *have we here?*
Dear, dear, oh *dear, dear, dear!*
   (Stabs self, dies in rhythm.)

KING:

Ah, me, see *what I've done,*
Life for *me* will *not be fun!*
My *reputation I must save,*
Guess I'll *join* them *in the grave!*
   (Chokes self with tie, in rhythm.)

EPILOGUE:

Thus ends our sad story,
We know the *ending's gory,*
Here's the *moral—it's not funny!*
You *can't* live on *love without money!*
I'll say good*bye to you,*
Guess I'd *better "cash in" too!*

   *(Shoots Self: BANG! BANG! BANG-BANG-BANG! and
   dies in rhythm.)*

The Crisis[22]

CHARACTERS: *Husband, and the doctor.*

HUSBAND *(rushing on stage and grabbing up the telephone):*
Get me Doctor N. O. Recovery, operator; this is an emergency. . . . Hello, Doctor! Come quick to *(local address)* at once! My wife is desperately sick, and I don't have her insurance paid up! Thanks, Doctor, I'll be waiting for you. Hurry, she's pretty sick!

There is an interlude of floor pacing, with appropriate mumbling, local news, perhaps a piece of celery taken out of pocketbook and eaten, or taking off shoes, switching socks, and replacing shoes.

Doctor rushes in with black bag.

HUSBAND: She's in there, Doc, and she's suffering so. Please help her. She's the only one who knows how to work our car jack.

DOCTOR *(steps into next room while husband paces some more. He returns):* Do you happen to have a stomach pump or a syphon?

HUSBAND: No, I don't, Doctor. Will anything else do?

DOCTOR: Well, get me a broom handle or a sink pump.

Is furnished with one and goes into room, while husband paces again.

DOCTOR: That didn't help. Quick, do you have a good saw or meat cleaver? Speed is important!

HUSBAND: Here's a saw, Doctor, but please do be careful. Is she pretty low, Doctor? Can she still talk? Ask her where she keeps my galoshes; it won't be long till winter.

DOCTOR: Can't be bothered just now, man. I have to get back; maybe this will help. We have no time to waste.

There is more floor pacing, perhaps a "True Story" maga-

[22] From J. Neal Griffith, Indiana, Pa.

zine sneaked out from under the rug for a surreptitious glance.

DOCTOR: That still didn't do it. I need a block and tackle, but if you don't have one a good piece of rope and an axe might work. Don't waste any time, man; time is of the essence!

HUSBAND: Here they are, doctor. Can't you tell me a little about the condition of the woman? She's the only wife I have just now, and it might take several months to replace her.

DOCTOR: Just be patient, mister. Maybe I'll have something to report in just a minute, but I can't talk just yet.

If former pacing has been across the stage, the husband tries a figure-eight pace this time, a waltz step, or a hop on each third step.

DOCTOR *(comes in calmly, mopping brow and looking quite pleased):* Well that's surely a relief. One of the most serious crises I have ever faced and I finally overcame all obstacles.

HUSBAND: Wonderful, Doctor. Will she be as well as ever? Will she be back on her feet in another month? Can we go on with our plans for our vacation next year?

DOCTOR: Oh, your wife! Well, yes, I must go back in to look at her. You said she was quite sick, didn't you? I'll be glad to look her over.

HUSBAND: But, Doctor! All those tools, and that rush. You said the crisis was over. Why can't you tell me how my wife is?

DOCTOR: You seem to have misunderstood. I haven't had a chance to look at your wife yet. The zipper of my doctor's bag was stuck, and I had a terrible time getting the thing open!

CURTAIN

That's It!

SCENE: *An army camp. Two soldiers are talking about a third.*

SCENE I

FIRST: Say, do you see that guy over there?

SECOND: The one picking up papers?

FIRST: Sure. He does that all the time.

SECOND: What for?

FIRST: I think he's nuts. He picks up a paper, looks at it, then shakes his head and picks up another.

SECOND: Let's go over to where he is.

FIRST: Sure.

They walk over, and sure enough he's picking up papers, shaking head sadly and saying, "That's not it."

SECOND: They humor him in the office. They will hand him some papers that don't mean anything. But he just looks at 'em and shakes his head.

FIRST: Well, they ought to let him out. Let's go to the PX. *(They leave.)*

SCENE II

SCENE: *The camp office. Two or three of office force plus camp commander present, plus our friend.*

FRIEND *(looking around the office at papers):* That's not it. *(At another)* That's not it.

COMMANDER: Private Notz, come here a minute.

Friend goes over.

COMMANDER: They sent back the results of that test you took the other day, and we have decided to let you go. Here are your discharge papers.

FRIEND *(looks carefully at the papers, then beams broadly):* That's it!

He leaves . . . as the others mutter, "He's not so dumb!"

BLACKOUT

Bawl Game

A girl comes on the stage crying. Soon another appears, then another, until there are several. A friend engages one in conversation.

"What's the matter with you girls?"

"We've been to a bawl game!"

"Bawl game? I don't understand. Did your team win?"

"It wasn't that kind of a bawl game. It was a crying game!"

"Crying game?"

"Yes . . . to see who could cry the best."

"Well, did you?"

"No . . . we lost. That's why . . . we're . . . bawling."

They all leave, still crying.

Kisses for Sale

A booth at a festival, with two pretty girls in it.

SALLY: This is fun, running this kissing booth.

DORIS: Sure it is. That's why I volunteered.

SALLY: Say, here comes your old flame, Jack Armstrong.

DORIS: Yeh . . . that all-American boy! He thinks he's it. I'll fix him.

Jack comes up to the booth.

JACK: Hello, girls. Well, I'm here.

SALLY: Yes, we see.

JACK: What have you got to offer?

DORIS: The sweetest kisses you ever had.

JACK: Are they worth my money?

DORIS: I think mine are. They're usually three for 50 cents, dear, but you can have four.

JACK: OK, you're on. *(Lays down 50 cents.)* Pucker up, kid.

DORIS: No, you pucker up. *(Reaches under the counter and gets candy kisses.)* You're the one that's winning. *(Turns back; he glares, leaves.)*

What a Night!

SCENE I

Romantic park scene by the lake or a stream in the moonlight in the summer, etc. He and she. Policeman looks on from some distance, reacts.

Policeman *(with keen delight):* Whatta night!

HE: Rosa! *(Sighs.)*

SHE: Reginald! *(Sighs.)*

HE: Beautiful! *(Sighs.)*

SHE: Yes . . . *(Sighs.)*

HE: Romantic!

SHE: Yes. . . .

HE: Love? *(Meaning himself.)*

SHE: Forever!

HE: Marry?

SHE: Dear!

HE: Happy.

SHE: Support?

HE: Papa.

SHE: Fine.

HE *(sighs):* Rosa!

SHE *(sighs):* Reginald!

COP: Well . . . that's where I came in! *(Leaves.)*

He and She continue to look in each other's eyes for BLACKOUT.

SCENE II

SCENE: *A deserted corn field. Two scarecrows. Winds.*
NARRATOR:

The North Wind howls *(calls* "Whooooooooooo!"*)*
The East Wind roars *(makes roaring sound.)*
The West Wind screeches *(makes screeching noise.)*
The South Wind blows *(say's* "Whooooo, you all!"*)*
Two scarecrows are discovered in this horrible weather.

FIRST SCARECROW: Sa-a-ay, did you ever see such weather?

SECOND: Sa-ay! It goes through me like a knife.

FIRST: I wish they'd take us in for the winter.

SECOND: Maybe they will pretty soon.

FIRST *(bending unusually far):* Sa-a-a-ay! *There* goes the *roof* off the farmer's barn.

SECOND: Who-o-o-o. Hold your hat!

FIRST: And THERE goes the barn!

SECOND: Who-o-o-o. *That* looks *bad!*

FIRST: What a night!

SECOND: Now we may stay here all winter.

FIRST: I'm like the weather man that moved to another place.

SECOND: How's that?

FIRST: The weather didn't agree with him.

North Wind comes whooping in, goes over to Second.

SECOND SCARECROW: Look out! Here I go somewhere else!
(Gets blown away.)

East Wind approaches the other: Goodbye.

FIRST SCARECROW: Here I go, too. What a night!

SCENE III

This scene uses four speakers. Each one starts over from the beginning when the previous one has gotten to the point marked with double asterisks (°°). Each delivers his lines in a melodramatic fashion, leaves the stage on completion, never paying attention either to other actors or to audience.

What a night! What a night!

'Twas a dark and stormy night, just outside the gates of Paris. I had my rusty, trusty pistol.

I aimed! I fired! My opponent fell into the arms of his second.°° What a night!

I rushed into a nearby cafe. A tall, dark gentleman approached me.

"I have killed a man," says I.

"Killed a man?" says he.

"Killed a man!" says I.

"What was his name?" says he.

"What was his name?" says I. "Zanzibar, that was his name."

"Zanzibar!" cried he. "Sir, you have killed my brother. We shall have to meet."

SCENE IV

SCENE: *A graveyard, very dimly lighted. For the punch idea, a strong rope or wire needs to be rigged up to pull one of the men up out of the deep "grave." Careful lighting can make this effective. Atmosphere music will help a lot.*

NARRATOR *(in dark, low tones):* My friends, you are about to witness an odd phenomenon. We are taking you to the bottom of a grave in the ——————— *(fill in name of a local cemetery)* cemetery. Joe Jackson *(or fill in name of a local person)* comes this way every night. There was a path at this spot, but now a grave has been dug across the path.

JOE JACKSON: Whatta night! Whatta night! *(Singing a bit unsteadily)* "Sweet Adeline . . . my Adeline" . . . *(Falls over the side into the grave.)* Whump! Sa-a-ay, what *is* this? Wuzzent here last night. *(Looks around.)* Maybe I kin jump out. *(Tries.)* Not here. Try over there. *(Goes over to another corner.)* Nope. Well, might as well go to sleep. *(Sits down, mutters.)* Whatta night! *(Snores.)*

NARRATOR: It looks as if Joe is in trouble. But wait. There is the sound of another coming down the path!

RED BAKER: Well, won't be long till I get home. Whatta night! No moon. Feller might break his neck on a night like this. *(Falls in, too.)* Whump! Where in the blasted tarnation am I? Huh. Must be a new grave. I'll try jumping. *(Tries a couple of corners.)* Huh. All tard out.

At that moment Joe Jackson stirs, moves over silently to where Red is.

JOE *(punching Red on the shoulder):* You can't get out of here!

Red jumps high, clears the wall, dashes away, screaming.

NARRATOR: But as you see, friends, he did.

BLACKOUT

Historical 4-D Television

This is an opportunity to go either forward or backward in the time span with 4-D Television. Prof. Dolittle has invented this new machine which puts ordinary 3-D color TV on the back shelf. It is "historic television" which can go back to any point in history, and forward to any future date.

Here are some uses for this device:

1. In school, as the setting for presenting several interesting historical scenes—military, political, social.
2. For a church group, the replaying of church history, including Biblical scenes.
3. For comedy in any situation, to take a look into the future, with interplanetary communication, magic rays, food pills, courtship, wonderful machines.
4. As the setting for a futuristic banquet or party or other social affair.
5. As the setting for a variety show, Year 2,500 style.

Converts

SCENE: *The parsonage, or manse. The minister and his wife.*

PASTOR: Well, I'm glad the meeting is over.

WIFE: You usually enjoy meeting with those business men, dear.

PASTOR: Yes, but now I am trying to get them to change their thinking.

WIFE: You're having trouble.

PASTOR: I tried to convince the people that the rich should share their wealth with the poor.

WIFE: That has always been the message. Weren't they convinced?

PASTOR: I guess you would say I was half-successful.

WIFE: What do you mean?

PASTOR: Well . . . so far I have convinced only the poor!

Water, Water![23]

SCENE: *The desert, at a water hole.*

Groans of a prospector come from a distance. He calls, "water-r-r-r." Gradually he crawls on stage, dragging himself.When he reaches the water hole he takes a dipper, drinks the water, spits out some, screams "POISON!" and drops.

The bucket has a little rice or confetti in the bottom and some water in the dipper, which is carefully replaced.

Other prospectors come in and drink, with the same results, each screaming "POISON!" and dropping. When the last one is just about to drink, the first one, supposedly dead, springs up and screams, "DON'T DRINK THAT WATER, IT'S POISON!" and grabs the bucket, hurling the contents out over the audience, who know that there is water in the dipper, and expect a bucketful on them!

(NOTE: for a build-up, an announcer could carefully explain about the problem of finding suitable water on the desert and spin a yarn about an experience of his. Also, a recording of the Sons of the Pioneers quartet, called "Water!" would bring in good atmosphere.)

Little Shot[24]

SCENE: *A grocery store. Older man for storekeeper.*

At the outset he mutters to himself, "This lumbago is jist

---

[23] From Buford and Betty Bush, Inverness, Calif.
[24] *Ibid.*

about a-killin' me. I shure wish I felt like I did when I was twenty-five! Well, guess I'd better straighten up. Here's some B-B shot. Kids jist don't buy 'em the way they used to. I'll put 'em up on the top shelf! *(Gets a ladder and painfully climbs to top shelf. If no shelf is available, he might leave them on top of the stepladder.)*

When he is finished, a boy comes in and wants to buy a nickel's worth of B-B's. The storekeeper climbs up the ladder painfully, climbs down again, sells to boy. A second boy comes in, wants some shot, so he clambers up again and gets the shot for the boy, comes down again, muttering to himself, and takes the money.

A third boy comes in. He looks at him and says, "Never mind, son, I know what *you* want," and climbs up for the third time, gets a package, brings it down, hands it to the boy. Boy is not completely pleased.

"Ain't that what you wanted, son?" asks the storekeeper.

"Sure, Mister Aiken," says the boy. "But I wanted *two* packages!"

Storekeeper faints.

Thought Waves[25]

The two "operators" indicate that they can pass numbers on to each other by mental telepathy.

Anyone from the audience may come up and write a number on the board. Then the assistant will speak to the Master Mind, who will immediately give out the number written.

Someone comes forward and writes, "4," whereupon the assistant gives the Master Mind four slaps on the back (with conversation to cover up) and he says, "Four."

Another comes up and writes "2" with the same result.

A stooge from the audience comes forward and writes, "00." The assistant looks very puzzled and doesn't seem to

25 *Ibid.*

know what to say. Then he "kicks" the Master Mind on the shins and makes some wild motions and the Master Mind says, "OO"! (Oh! Oh!)

The Paper Read Aloud

Three or four persons are sitting on the stage or are observed, reading the paper. One snickers, starts to tell a joke. Another interrupts, reading from the gossip column (some local news), and another begins to tell about a bargain he saw in the paper. They read louder and talk louder. Finally they all leave in a huff, glaring at each other. Then the joke teller returns and finishes telling his joke. *(It should be a good one.)*

Sweet Mystery[26]

SCENE: *Somewhere in an army camp. Sergeant, Mrs. Gushalot, men.*

NARRATOR: My friends, we bring you this story for whatever it is worth. We cannot absolutely vouch for its accuracy, but we think you will be interested because it was such a long, valiant search that Mrs. Gushalot carried on in order that she might thank personally one who had done her such a great favor. And here is our sketch. We hope you like it.

MRS. GUSHALOT: Oh, sergeant, I know I am not supposed to be here . . .

SERGEANT: No, lady, you ain't.

MRS. G: But I'm on an unusual mission and need your help.

SERGEANT: What is it, lady?

MRS. G: You know about Mr. Rhee, of Korea?

SERGEANT: Sure.

MRS. G: Do you know that his son is a photographer for *Life* Magazine?

[26] From Bill Wilson, Birmingham, Ala.

SERGEANT *(impatiently)*: Naw.

MRS. G: Well, he is . . . and he is the sweetest thing. He did me the most wonderful favor, and I want to repay him! I've heard he's here.

SERGEANT: Now that you mention it, I think he *is* here.

MRS. G: Oh, if I could only see him. I want to thank him and give him something of my appreciation.

SERGEANT: Sure, ma'am. Come with me.

MRS. G: *(looking off stage at the supposed Mr. Rhee, Junior)*: There he is. There he is. Ah, sweet, Mr. Rhee, of *Life*, at *last* I've found thee!"

Rubber

A baby has been left in his carriage outside a store. Two persons of great dignity of speech and position are viewing it.

FIRST: I say, Smithkins, what a baby!

SECOND: Tomkins, you are right. *What* a baby!

FIRST: It looks like my Aunt Agatha!

SECOND: In truth, it does.

FIRST: And I always thought Aunt Agatha was the ugliest woman I ever saw.

SECOND: There's no disputing!

Both are staring at the child in fascinated horror when its mother comes out. She sees them, and with strong feeling, utters the single word, "RUBBER!" contemptuously at both of them and leaves.

FIRST *(to Second, after a pause)*: Thank heavens, what a relief. I was thinking it might be real!

Bum's Rush

LEADER: Friends, we want to give you a little skit here now. It just involves two of our number, but we thought you would enjoy it. One of the characters could be called a "panhandler." I have a cousin who is a panhandler—he is an intern over at the local hospital. But *this man* is just a bum. As our scene opens, he approaches another man on the street:

BUM: Say, mister, could I have a moment of your time?
MAN: What do you want with it?
BUM: Would you gimme two bits for a bed?
MAN: Hummmmm! Maybe. Let's see the bed first!

Bum looks at him peculiarly and walks off. Man grins, walks on down the street.

Letter Carrier[27]

SCENE: *The prison. Two prisoners are seen at opposite sides of the stage. Each of them has on striped clothes. They have their heads down and only speak to each other as they pass.*

"Hey."
"Hey."
"Who are you?"
"Slug. Who're you?"
"Blackie."
"How long you in?"
"Life. How long for you?"
"Twenty years."
"Do something for me?"
"Depends."
"No trouble."
"O K . . . what?"
"Mail this letter when you get out."

27 From Buford and Betty Bush, Inverness, Calif.

chapter 4

CAN

DO

THIS?

feats
forfeits and initiation stunts

CAN YOU DO THIS?

WHEN IT IS TIME for initiations, or when the group are just standing around, or when they are sitting at the table between courses, often it is fun to have a filler to demonstrate or suggest.

Here is a variety of physical feats, tricks, easy contests of skill, to fit into those very situations and many others. Many would be good at parties. This section has much material especially designed for boys and men.

Go through the entire section and mark those which appeal to you.

FEATS

Balance the Feather

Can you balance a feather on your nose?

Throw Ping-Pong Ball

Can you throw a ping-pong ball the greatest distance? Measure distance for each player.

Curving Ping-Pong Ball

If you throw a ping-pong ball hard with a straight, forward motion, but let it roll off the forefinger and middle finger, the ball will curve upward, especially near the end of its flight.

Swing the Bell

Can you swing a bell without ringing it?

Candle Blow

Set up candles in any formation—square, circle, triangle—and from a given distance see who can blow out the most.

Squeezing Seeds

When served watermelon or other melon, see who can snap or squeeze seeds and make them go the greatest distance. (Don't forget to make "watermelon false teeth" from the rinds! Just cut out some outlandish teeth and insert in the mouth between lip and gums.)

Swat Him

With a swatter made from a cloth-stuffed sock, each of the two opponents tries to swat the other while in a burlap sack.

Blindfold Swat

Same idea as Swat Him, but each person is blindfolded. The group will enjoy this.

Find the Clock

Blindfold a person and see how long it takes him to find a hidden clock. Have several contestants, keep them out of the area where the clock is to be hidden, hide the clock in the same place every time, bring them in one at a time to try their luck. A watch with a second hand records the time required for each person.

Who Touched Me?

When a player is blindfolded, have him guess who touched him, or who made that noise.

Friendly Blindfold

Have two persons, blindfolded, try to walk up to each other and shake hands. Try many pairs in the group to see if they can do it.

Big Hold

See how many beans you can hold between your fingers. See who in the entire group can hold the most.

Testing Water

The prospectors were searching for fresh water. (Go on with the story.) They did not want to taste it, for they would become thirstier if it were salt water. So they tested it the way I am going to. (Have some glasses of salt water and fresh water brought out. You can indicate the salt water because an egg floats in it but sinks in the fresh.)

Sweetness and Lye

Have two matches representing a boy and a girl. Indicate that a touch of lye (soap) on the water on which the matches are floating, will turn them away from each other, but a bit of sugar will make them come together.

Making a Glass Sing

Tempered glass of the cut-glass variety will usually "sing" if you will wet your finger and run it around the rim.

Touch Floor Backward

Can you stand, bend backward, and touch the floor with your hands?

Jumping, Feet to Hands

Can you jump continuously from feet to hands, alternately spreading and closing your feet and hands?

Circles

Can you make circles with the right hand on the table in one direction and with a foot on the floor in an opposite direction?

Tricky Writing

Can you move beans from one circle on the table to another with one hand and write your name with the other?

Hop and Turn

Can you place one foot against the wall, then hop over it with the other foot, doing a half-turn in the process?

Hopping Hats

Have a row of hats. Each person hops over the first one forward, second backward, and so on, picking last hat up in mouth and tossing it backward overhead.

Stand a Minute

Can you balance for a full minute on one foot—blindfolded, or with eyes closed?

Thread the Needle

Can you balance on one knee and thread a needle?

Kick the Ball

Try tossing up a basketball so that it lands behind you, kick it with feet.

Dog Jump

Can you jump over a stick held in the hands, or through your clasped hands?

Pick Up Chair

Make a toe line 2 feet from wall, with a chair between. Lean forward, put head against the wall, pick up chair, and recover your balance.

Water Toter

Carry a glass or pan full of water across the room or for several paces, without spilling any.

Pick Up Magazine

Stand on one foot, hold other behind, lean forward, and pick up a magazine in teeth. (It could be the magazine of the organization.)

Dropping Marbles

Hold them waist high, see who can drop the most into a bottle or small can.

Jump Your Toe

Holding toes of either foot in the hand, can you jump the free foot over the held one without letting go?

Pulling Out the Napkin

With a bottle on a napkin on the table, can you take the napkin from under the bottle without touching bottle or knocking it over? Rap the table hard enough to bounce bottle up, gradually pulling out the napkin each time?

Salt Shaker Standing on Side

Can you make a hexagonal-shaped salt shaker stand on its side at a 45 degree angle? This is possible by pouring a small pile of salt on the table and working the shaker, set at a 45 degree angle, down until it is about one salt grain of thickness from the table. It may take several tries, but it definitely can be done.

Putting Coin into Cup

There is a coin in front of a cup standing on a table. Can you put the coin in the cup without touching the coin? Yes, by striking the table underneath the coin, thus making the coin land in the cup.

Coin Catch

Put several coins on your elbow, held out shoulder high with palm down. Try to drop coins off the elbow and catch them in the same hand. To make it harder, spread them out on the elbow.

Balloon Blow

With the second hand of a watch, see who can keep a balloon (or feather) in the air the longest.

Kneel, and Lift Chair

Can you kneel on your right knee at the side of a chair, take the lower end of back leg in your right hand and lift the chair from the floor? (Make these "left" if left-handed.)

Putting Cork into Bottle

With a bottle on the floor, cork sitting loosely in place, stand on one foot and try to hop, pushing down the cork into bottle with that same foot. (The foot bearing your weight is the one to push in the cork.)

Croquet First

With the second hand of a watch, see who can make the regular rounds of a croquet court in the least time.

Miniature Golf, Fast

Do the same with a miniature golf course laid out, with small balls or golf balls, hockey sticks for golf sticks. The winner completes in shortest time.

Sticky Glass

Cup your palm over a full glass of water, then suddenly straighten out your fingers. The glass will adhere to the palm.

Curvy Blow

Put a lighted candle behind a bottle. Blow on the other side of the bottle and put the light out.

Making Egg Stand on End

You can make a hard-boiled egg stand in an upright position on a plate by making small horizontal circles with the plate.

Figure Magic

Have people take any even number, multiply it by 3, divide that by 2, multiply by 3. To give them the answer, ask how many times 9 will go into it, double what they give you, and you have the answer!

Reverse Actions

Can you obey instructions in reverse, or give wrong answers. This is fun to try on a group.

Eleven Matches Make Nine

Who can place 6 matches, side by side, add 5 more and make 9? You spell out, "NINE."

Blindfold Drawing

While blindfolded, can you draw a picture of a girl on the blackboard?

Singing Backward

Who can sing "America, the Beautiful," backward? (Turn your back to the audience and sing.)

Touching a Book

Can you touch a book outside and inside without opening it? (Yes, outdoors and indoors!)

Palm Read in Five Seconds

After giving this a build-up, put a drop of mercurochrome or a red chalk mark in the middle of the person's hand.

Jump a Pencil

Can you put a pencil on the floor, stand with toes almost touching it, toes grasped in hands, and jump over it?

Raise the Broom

Try taking a broom in your right hand (left if you are left-handed) and from the far end, work it up until you have the "broom end."

CAN YOU DO THIS?

Turn the Glass

With your right elbow at your side, palm up, put a full glass of water on your hand; see if you can swing hand around underneath armpit and complete the turn without spilling water.

Coin Turn Trick

Can you put a coin on your little finger and do the same thing, without dropping the coin?

Hand Slap

One player has hands extended, palms up. The other has his hands extended, palms down toward those of first player. The "palms up" player takes the aggressive, trying to slap the backs of the hands of his opponent without warning. The opponent, of course, tries to get his hands out of the way. Reverse after a while.

Coin Grab

One person has a coin in his palm with hand open. He is to try to close palm and keep coin, while the other, who starts with his hand, palm down, about 6 inches above, tries to grab the coin. By making a quick "slapping motion," thus forcing coin to jump, he will get it nearly every time.

Pull Them Apart

Can you pull apart the hands of a player who has his elbows out to his sides, tips of middle fingers touching at his chest?

Bull Ring

Name it what you like, but draw a circle a few feet in diameter, and see if you can pull your opponent into the ring, he (the bull) resisting.

Ball Wrestle

One person holds a volleyball or basketball or other ball of that size. The other tries to wrest it from him. May be timed.

Wrist Wrestle

Two players interlace fingers. The object is to force your opponent to his knees.

Back Bend

Place a crumpled piece of paper about 25 to 30 inches behind your heels. Kneel on both knees, arms on chest, and see if you can lean over backward and get the paper (or handkerchief) in your teeth.

Tying the Calf

Two players, with shoes off, have ropes, and in two minutes or less are trying at the same time to tie up opponent's ankles but to keep from being tied. It's rough!

Buzz

Three players stand side by side, firmly braced with wide stance, the middle one with hat on. Each outside player has his outside hand to his face, fingers directed toward center player, who will later try to slap those fingers. The inside arm of each player is free. The center one starts buzzing, first one and then the other, tantalizing. Finally he strikes— by slapping the hand of one of the players (near his face). This player may then (and not before) try to knock the hat off the center one. If so, he goes to center.

Some Self-Testing Actions[1]

Take ten steps forward on a straight line.

Jump into air and clap feet together once.

[1] From Harry D. Edgren, George Williams College, Chicago, Ill.

Lie flat on floor, arms folded, and come up to sitting position.

Arms folded behind back, kneel on both knees and get up without losing balance.

Push up three times.

Squat position, hands crossed in front of body, jump to a stride with hands horizontal sideward.

Make a full pirouette to left.

Jump into air and clap feet together twice.

Stand on right foot, grasp left foot behind right knee, bend and touch left knee to the floor, and stand up without losing balance.

Hold toes of either foot in opposite hand, jump up with free foot over foot that is held, without letting it go.

Jump into air and slap both heels behind your back with your hands.

Stand and kick the right foot shoulder high.

Stand on left foot, bend forward, and place both hands on the floor, raise right leg, stretch it back, touch head to floor, and return to standing position.

Stand with both feet together, bend down, hands between legs around outside of ankles, and hold fingers together in front of ankles for five seconds.

Make full pirouette to the right.

Kneel on both knees, sit down, and get up without unfolding arms.

Stand on left foot, hold bottom of right foot against inside of left knee for ten seconds, eyes closed.

Take frog stand position.

Stand on left foot, sit down on left heel, and stand up again.

Push away from the wall.

Jump and reach, make highest mark.

FORFEITS AND INITIATION STUNTS

Several of those already given would be suitable for forfeits and initiations, especially for boys. Here are some other suggestions:

1. Tongue twisters. (Make them read these three times.)
   Six gray geese on green grass grazing.
   Six thick thistle sticks.
   Round and round the rugged rock the ragged rascal ran.
   Copper coffee pot.
   Ziggy Jazinski.
2. Sing a song (perhaps a lullaby).
3. Yawn until somebody in the group yawns, too.
4. Read or say something funny without laughing.
5. Put your hand where the other hand can't reach it (on the elbow).
6. Say a number of complimentary things about yourself.
7. With one hand, move a number of beans one by one from one dish to another. (Between two, this could be a race.)
8. Fill a glass with water, using a thimble (could be a race).
9. Put a number of marbles in a milk bottle, with a fork.
10. Pile up twelve tin cans without letting them fall.